BUYING INSURANCE

BUYING INSURANCE

MAXIMUM PROTECTION AT MINIMUM COST

Wilson J. Humber

MOODY PRESS

CHICAGO

ISBN: 0-8024-1212-2

1 3 5 7 9 10 8 6 4 2

Printed in the United States of America

Contents

SAVE ON YOUR INSURANCE

Take a moment to add up how much insurance costs you.

If you keep track of your expenses, you have probably noticed an increase in the cost of your insurance over the past few years. Medical insurance has tripled in price the last ten years. My car insurance jumped 40 percent the day we added our oldest son as an occasional driver. Your salary continuation policy at work increases an average of 20 percent in every five year period, and if you followed the advice of your insurance agent your cost for life insurance would rise several thousand dollars. If you buy a new VCR, the salesperson will try to sell you extended warranties. When you buy a car, the finance person tries to sell you car insurance and a service contract. If you resist, here comes a credit life and disability sales pitch. Look into refinancing your home and they bring up mortgage insurance. Do you feel badgered and pressured into having to say no, too many times, to buying more insurance?

This booklet is designed to help you analyze and determine your needs for all types of insurance and to help you learn to buy *adequate protection at minimal cost*. When you finish this material, you will know how to cut 25 to 50 percent off what you currently pay for insurance without sacrificing necessary coverage. If your current cost for all insurance is $3,000 to $6,000 per year that means savings of $750 to $3,000 per year. The time you spend reading and applying this material could be worth $150/hour or more to you!

As a Christian you certainly want to know what the Bible says about the matter. Is buying insurance scriptural? Does purchasing insurance reflect a lack of faith in God's protection or provision? The word *insurance* is not used in the Bible, but the principles of planning for the future and providing for yourself and your family are found throughout Scripture. As believers we accept both the sovereignty of God and our own personal responsibility. It is our responsibility to plan for the future and practice good stewardship with the assets God has provided for us to manage. It is our responsibility to provide for ourselves and our families. Christ made clear our responsibility to plan wisely for the future when He said, "For which one of you, when he wants to build a tower, does not first sit down and calculate the cost, to see if he has enough to complete it? Otherwise, when he has laid a foundation, and is not able to finish, all who observe it begin to ridicule him, saying, 'This man began to build and was not able to finish'" (Luke 14:28–30). Regarding providing for yourself and your family Paul says, "But if anyone does not provide for his own, and especially for those of his household, he has denied the faith, and is worse than an unbeliever" (1 Timothy 5:8). Notice the word is "provide" not "protect."

AVOIDING EXTREMES

If we are to live by biblical principles, we must avoid two extremes. First, we should not attempt to "protect" ourselves and our families from every emergency, loss, disaster, or contingency that could occur. That would be an attempt on our part to function independent of God. His wishes are for us to remain dependent upon Him, abiding in Him, and focused on Him. If we attempted to insure or protect ourselves and our families against any and all perils, the cost would be prohibitive or would greatly stress or hamper a balanced, total spending plan. The second extreme to avoid is abrogation of any and all personal responsibility by saying, "I don't need insurance—my trust is in God." That is neither faith nor trust but presumption and foolishness. When Jesus was tempted the second time by Satan, to jump off the top of the temple, Satan misquoted Scripture to prove his challenge. Jesus replied, "You shall not put the Lord your God to the test" (Matthew 4:7). What we seek is a balance between overinsuring and not having insurance at all. Our purpose here is to help you find and select adequate protection without paying too much for it.

Although insurance can be defined as surrendering a part of current resources (income) to offset potential future loss, I prefer to define insurance as protection against large, unpredictable losses of a few, with the small, guaranteed loss of many. For example, take a group of 100 men, all age fifty-five. Statistics tell us that on the average one of these 100 men will die before reaching age fifty-six. If each man put $150 into an insurance pool, the pool would have $15,000. By contract, the pool would agree to pay the net proceeds to the survivors of the man who died. This is how all insurance policies work. A portion of the $15,000 would go to the salesman of the policies, $3,000 in our example. Part of the proceeds would go to pay the overhead of the insurance, let's say $1,000. The largest part of the premiums would be paid out to the policy's beneficiaries, the survivors of the man who died. If $10,000 were paid to the beneficiaries, $1,000 would remain for "profit" of the insurance company. What we have are 99 men with small losses ($150) to pay large benefits ($10,000) to the few who lose through death, disability, accident, or illness. This booklet will help you limit your losses (premiums) and free your money for better use. Our goal is to help you cut expenses without giving up necessary provision for you and your family.

PROBABILITY OF A CLAIM

Principle: Buy insurance based on the probability of a claim.

In any year you are more likely to have a medical claim than you are to be disabled. The odds of being disabled are higher than the probability of a loss to your car or home. A claim for damage or loss to your car or home is more likely than the chance of your death. Thus, we should allocate resources as follows:

1. Major Medical
2. Disability Income
3. Property and Casualty (home and auto)
4. Life Insurance
5. Other Insurance

If you only have enough income to buy two policies, use that income to protect yourself and your family from your two greatest risks: major medical and disability. We will proceed to study each area to help you determine necessary coverage then give you ideas to help you purchase that coverage at minimum cost. Let's begin by examining priority number one.

MEDICAL INSURANCE

Fortunately, for most of us medical insurance is provided by our employers. You may have heard that there are 37 million people in the U.S. who have no medical insurance. What follows pertains to three groups, those with group medical, those with no coverage, and those who find and purchase individual policies. In the past twenty years the price of medical coverage has increased dramatically and will, for a number of reasons, continue to increase in cost, decrease in benefits, or both. Good coverage is expensive, but it is a necessity for each of us. A single claim for an accident, disease, or illness can cost tens of thousands of dollars. The cost from an auto accident, cancer, or bypass surgery can wipe out everything you have accumulated or will accumulate during your lifetime.

Principle: Buy comprehensive medical insurance now.
Regardless of the healthcare programs that may be proposed or passed by Congress, you should secure private comprehensive medical insurance for yourself and your family. The one certainty in all government programs is change. Don't wait for the government to act or amend its medical programs; if you do not have individual comprehensive medical insurance, now is the time to purchase it.

Failure to do so is like playing Russian roulette. If you continue to play, sooner or later you will release the firing pin on the chamber containing the bullet. It is our personal responsibility to provide adequate protection against the potential large losses from medical problems.

Many types of policies are available: hospital expense, surgical expense, physician's expense, major medical, HMOs, PPOs, and others. The coverage can be very narrow—policies that cover hospital expense only but not surgical, physician, and other expenses, or very broad—policies like comprehensive major medical that cover hospital, surgical, physician, and most other medical expenses. The medical industry today is evolving, but the types of coverage vary further by the type of contract you purchase.

Health Maintenance Organizations (HMOs) offer total care. You pay a regular premium plus a small charge for office visits, and all your health problems are handled. You never have to fill out claim forms, and in theory, HMOs are cheaper than competing policies. I say in theory, because you get less treatment than from a traditional medical practice. HMOs cut costs by using an HMO doctor and requesting fewer diagnostic tests, fewer referrals to outside specialists, and fewer hospital stays. You may feel that HMOs undertreat, but perhaps traditional doctors overtreat or overtest. People either love or hate HMOs; there is very little in-between. For more detailed advice, get "Choosing an HMO: An Evaluation Checklist" free from Fulfillment, American Association of Retired Persons, 1909 K Street N.W., Washington, DC 20049.

Check out a *preferred-provider organization (PPO)*. These plans are available from a number of companies including Blue Cross/Blue Shield. Generally, coverage should be less expensive, but you are restricted to doctors who have joined the plan and specialists to whom they refer patients. Since these plans usually charge by age, sex, and geographic area, the price is a bargain for the unhealthy but more costly for the very healthy.

Check out *managed care* or *utilization review* policies. They are subject to the same rules as many company group plans: mandatory second opinions, permission prior to non-emergency surgery, and limits on hospital stays. In some states these plans are available as riders to some Blue Cross/Blue Shield plans. In return for these restrictions you get a lower cost than *Indemnity Major Medical* plans.

There are two types of Indemnity plans. *Service benefits* covers a fixed percentage of each bill subject to certain limits, and *indemnity benefits* pays a set sum toward each bill. "We pay 85% of the cost of a semi-private room" is a "service benefit." "We pay $190 per day if you are hospitalized" is an "indemnity benefit." Service benefits cost more because they cover more, but you are free to choose your own doctor.

Regardless of the type of medical insurance you have, here are some guidelines to help you lower your cost:

Guideline 1: Choose a higher deductible to lower your cost, and save the difference in premium. Here's a chart of premiums (cost) for a thirty-five-year-old couple with two children for a service benefit comprehensive major medical plan.

DEDUCTIBLE	COST	SAVINGS	PERCENT SAVED
$250	$4,435	-0-	0%
500	3,229	$1,116	25%
1,000	2,329	2,016	46%
2,500	1,729	2,616	60%
10,000	717	3,628	83%

The savings in cost from a $250 deductible to a $1,000 deductible is 46%; that's $2,016 per year, or $168/month. If you raised your deductible from $250 to $1,000 and saved the $168/month difference in premium, you would have saved $1,008 in only six months, $2,520 in fifteen months, and $10,080 in five years. Having these amounts accumulated would enable you to take even higher deductibles of $2,500 to $10,000 and further lower your costs.

Remember our goal of adequate protection at minimum cost. Take higher deductibles and save the premiums, or use the savings to retire high-interest debt like 18% on your credit cards.

Guideline 2: Cut costs by selecting higher coinsurance. In addition to the set deductible, there is a cost known as coinsurance. After paying the deductible, you are still responsible for 10 to 30% of the next $3,000 to $10,000 in charges, depending on your particular policy. For example, you have a $1,000 deductible policy with a 15% coinsurance to $5,000. On a $15,000 claim, you pay your $1,000 deductible, plus $750 coinsurance on the next $5,000, plus you pay nothing on the remaining $9,000. You paid $1,750; the policy covered $13,250. If you elected a 30% coinsurance to $5,000, you would cut your costs of the policy 22% or $512/year. That's your savings for risking $750 more on the same $15,000 claim.

In calculating both the deductible you are willing to cover and the percentage and limit of coinsurance, look carefully at your saving or your IRA accounts, which are accessible without penalty if you encounter a large medical expense. If you have faithfully funded your IRA $2,000/year for the past seven years, you have $14,000+ salted away. Even after taxes that's enough for you to consider the $10,000 deductible, saving you 83% of the price of the $250 deductible or $3,628/year. In less than three years, you would save more than your $10,000 deductible. Of course, if you have a major medical bill within those three years, you have spent more rather than saving more; calculating your risk against your potential savings is part of wise stewardship of resources.

Guideline 3: Read your policy carefully to determine what you are and are not covered against. Don't assume everything is covered, only to be shocked when you learn the hard way what isn't covered. For example, does your contract cover:

(1) full cost of basic hospital services: semi-private room (private room you pay), emergency room, nurses, medicines, X-rays, and lab tests?

(2) full cost of surgery including anesthesia and outpatient?

(3) your children, including infants at birth? stepchildren? foster children?

(4) doctor bill in full? in part? subject to what limits?

(5) prescription drugs? subject to what limits, if any?

(6) mental problems? substance abuse?

(7) pre-existing conditions? starting when?

(8) the cost of dental surgery? endonics? periodontics? impacted wisdom teeth?

(9) incidental expenses: private nurse, physical therapy, oxygen, pacemakers, and other medical devices?

(10) A $500,000 or higher maximum lifetime benefit? (if not, consider raising it).

If you can answer these questions, you have either done your homework or have had your share of medical problems. If you can't answer the questions, find out what you are and are not covered for now while you can change things (after a claim it is too late).

Guideline 4: Understand maternity benefits and limits. Did you know that: there is a $3,000 to $5,000 maximum benefit on pregnancies? the cost for maternity benefits is $200/month? you still pay the deductible and the coinsurance? there is a nine- to twelve- month waiting period before coverage begins? If you are planning on a child, you are generally better off saving the $200/month than buying a maternity benefit option. If there are complications after birth, the child is covered if the existing policy covers the mother (at least six months before the due date). If you aren't sure, do your homework.

Guideline 5: Don't waste money on dental, accident, prescription drugs, disease policies, student policies, hospital income, or policies sold on TV, mail order, or in the newspaper. Dental insurance costs about $500 per year, has a maximum benefit of $1,000, and carries a $50 to $100 deductible. Dental coverage sounds attractive and logical, but don't make emotional, rather than logical, decisions and waste your money (on insurance premiums). You are probably covered for oral surgery under the surgical section of your basic policy, and almost no dental policy covers orthodontics, root canals, impacted wisdom teeth, or periodontics. There may be exceptions, but you can cut your cost by avoiding dental coverage.

Accident coverage is a high-profit and low-risk policy for the insurance company. Excluding accidents on the job, covered by workman's compensation, less than 10% of claims come from accidents. Consider cutting the option and cutting your cost.

Unless you have a chronic illness that requires continual medication costing over $100/month, save your money and skip coverage for prescription drugs. Avoid "one disease" policies like cancer and heart attack policies; they are poor buys. If possible, cover dependent children on your policy rather than with a separate student policy. Don't waste money on hospital income policies; the benefits are tiny but the cost isn't.

Guideline 6: Buy from top-rated, safe companies with good service. The best way to find good value is still word of mouth referral, but to determine the safety of any insurance company requires a little homework. Up until 1980 it would not have been necessary to discuss safety. Even during the great depression of 1929 to 1933, when almost nine thousand banks failed, not a single insurance company went under or failed to provide benefits as promised. In the last few years we have seen the Savings & Loan debacle, and dozens of large companies have gone into extinction, merged, or been forced into bankruptcy. Claims and losses have never been worse than 1993–94: the earthquakes in California, Hurricane Andrew that hit Florida and the gulf states, and the midwestern flood. The insurance industry lost $45 billion. Only a decade ago AIDS and HIV tests were unheard of, but today AIDS looms like the black plague for thousands of people, representing untold billions in final claims. Deal with only top-rated companies. If you want to shave corners to save a few dollars this is not the place to do it.

Buy from companies with high quality ratings from at least three of the five insurance-rating companies.

A. M. Bests	A+	*to*	A++
Standard & Poor	AA+	*to*	AAA
Moody's	Aaa1	*to*	Aaa
Duff & Phelps	AA+	*to*	AAA
Weiss	A	*to*	A+

Study the following summary carefully:

(1) If possible insure with your employer or group plan offered by your professional association, group, or union.

(2) Buy coverage now while you are healthy. This is particularly important in changing jobs, divorce, or death of a spouse. If necessary convert your group coverage or buy a short-term policy. Don't go naked!

(3) Make sure your lifetime benefit is between $500,000 and $1,000,000.

(4) If you're female, look for a unisex rate (it's cheaper for you).

(5) Beware of low-priced policies. If it looks too good to be true it probably is.

(6) If you can pass a medical exam, take one; it will cut your cost.

(7) Consider service benefit rather than indemnity benefit contracts.

(8) Insist on a policy that is guaranteed renewable at your option.

(9) Get coverage now and keep it. After a problem, it is very expensive if it's available at all.

(10) Don't lie on the application or omit facts. The Medical Information Bureau (MIB) has a ream of medical information already in your file. I just watched a widow pay a $75,000 medical bill from a $100,000 life policy because her husband lied on

the application and omitted material facts. The insurance company refunded her premiums. They could have kept them, sued her, and won for his behavior. Remember our goal: adequate protection at minimal cost. Seek the balance between no coverage and spending too much to "protect" yourself from any and every loss.

You now know 95% of everything you need to know about medical insurance. If you don't have coverage, act now. If you have coverage, use these ideas to reduce your costs. One final principle: *To save money on any insurance shop and compare costs and benefits,* although you should not buy insurance from a company that is not highly rated, even to save costs.

DISABILITY INCOME

You probably have life insurance, medical insurance, auto insurance, and even some insurance on your furniture and personal property, but have you forgotten your single largest asset—your earning power? Disability income is priority number two in your list of needs.

The chart on page 23 shows your cumulative income starting at various ages and assuming you work until your sixty-seventh birthday. Income is $24,000 per year and is adjusted for inflation at 3% per year (column 3). Column 2 is a cumulative fixed income. A thirty-two-year-old who works thirty-five years at $24,000/year will earn $840,000 during his working years. If his income increased 3% per year, $1,456,090 will pass through his hands. Indeed your largest asset is your earning power.

CUMULATIVE INCOME

AGE	CUMULATIVE INCOME	INCREASING @ 3% PER YEAR
22	$1,080,000	$2,225,279
32	840,000	1,456,090
42	600,000	875,021
52	360,000	445,200
62	120,000	127,420

What if you are a thoracic surgeon, age thirty-eight, earning $350,000 per year when you lose three fingers on your right hand in a hunting accident? You may have a disability income policy bought ten years ago that pays you $2,500 per month, but you are not eligible for social security. When you do your budget you find your expenses are $200,000/year. What do you do now? Maybe you are an advertising salesperson, age forty-eight, earning $80,000/year when years of cumulative stress, pressure, and deadlines lead to a massive heart attack that leaves you unable to return to your pressure cooker full-time sales job. Your three children, two in college and one in a private school, are a heavy

23

burden, but the real shock is when your social security claim is denied. What do you do now? What if you were thirty, widowed and struggling as a single parent but surviving as a supervisor with a $28,000 wage to support yourself and your three children when an auto accident leaves you handicapped for life? You check your employee benefits and find your salary runs six weeks then stops. Just as bad, the other driver, who was cited for DUI, has no insurance, no license, and no assets. What would you do if an accident, illness, disease, or medical problem destroyed your earning power?

There are seven possible safety nets between you and disaster: social security, workman's compensation, company/group coverage, personal assets, a working spouse, your family, and personal disability income insurance. Your social security can provide income six months after you are disabled if the disability is permanent or total (no help for the surgeon or the salesman above and perhaps the single parent). The amount you can collect on social security depends on your past wages and family circumstances, but be aware that 80% of the claims for disability are denied. Even with an attorney, less than 10% of the originally denied claims are reversed. At best, your benefit will be $1,200/month plus a reduced benefit for dependent children.

Workman's compensation, mandatory employer provided coverage, covers you for accident, injury, or damage you incur at or during your work. Some companies offer group coverage called salary continuation or disability income, but generally these benefits are short term (six months or less). Safety net number four is your personal assets. If, for example, you have $20,000 tucked away into IRAs, $60,000 in savings, and $120,000 from an inheritance, that $200,000 total could earn you $1,000/month if it were invested at 6% interest. Safety nets number five and six are a working spouse and/or help from your family. Your final safeguard from disaster is a personal disability income policy that pays you monthly income, starting some time after your disability and continuing for some specified period of time.

HOW MUCH DO YOU NEED?

How much coverage you need is an individual question that can be answered by determining exactly how much money it would take for you to live on. If today you are earning $3,000 per month, after taxes and other deductions your take-home pay might be $30,000/year or $2,500/month. A small part of your living expense might be eliminated if you were disabled instead of working (business lunches, transportation, and clothing, for example). Then there are the luxuries you could do without like cable TV, meals out, and pocket money. After squeezing your budget, perhaps your expenses could be shaved down to $2,000/month survival income. To be safe add back $200 to $300/month for the extra expenses necessary for a disabled person to survive. Now you have five sources of income.

SOURCE	AMOUNT	BENEFIT PERIOD & CONDITIONS
1. Social Security	$0–1,200/ month	Six-month wait, benefits to age 65
2. Workman's Comp.	Varies	Varies by state
3. Company Coverage	Varies	Varies by company
4. Income from Assets	Varies	Varies by individual
5. Working Spouse	Varies	Varies by couple
6. Help from Family	Varies	Varies by individual

You need to complete your own calculations. For example, let's say your only source of income was social security, which amounted to $1,000/month. Your necessary disability income is the difference between the *total sources of income* ($1,000/month) and your necessary survival income. If your survival income is $2,300, you need $1,300/month in disability income. A general guideline is to purchase 75% of your gross income less potential social security benefits and sources of income unique to you. If your income is under $30,000/year the percentage guideline rises to 80%, and if your income is over $50,000/year the percentage guideline drops to 60 to 65%. For very high earners the maximum benefit drops to 50 to 60% of income.

In calculating your amount of disability income, don't forget about taxes. Today social security benefits are taxed at 50% or more if your taxable income exceeds $25,000 for singles or $32,000 for marrieds. Workman's compensation is generally not taxable, but company paid salary continuation, like your salary, is fully taxed if the company paid the premium. If you pay the premium, then the benefits are generally non-taxable. Income from assets can be fully taxable to tax-free depending on the particular investments selected. Income from a working spouse is taxable, but after certain limits the expenses of your disability may be an itemized medical deduction. If your family is a source of income you can figure that income would also be free of tax if you received less than $10,000/year per family member helping. Last, your personal disability income is tax-free if you paid the premiums. If your employer paid the premiums or reimbursed you for the cost, then the benefits you get are taxed as ordinary income.

To review, first determine a survival budget. Second, determine your sources of potential income (see page 26). Third, decide the amount of benefits you need. The bad news is that disability income, just like major medical insurance, is expensive. The good news is that those expenses can be reduced.

CUTTING THE COST

The cost for disability income is a function of your age, health, occupation, elimination period, benefit amount, and benefit period. You can't change your age, and I would not suggest changing jobs just to reduce the cost of insurance, but you can reduce your cost of insurance by working at improving your health. If you are a smoker—STOP! It will save you close to $1,000/year on cigarettes and reduce your costs for all types of insurance. If you are overweight, diet and exercise. You can cut costs 20% if you qualify for preferred rates. Finally, decide to get adequate rest.

Principle: Take long elimination periods to cut costs.
An elimination period is the delay between the onset of disability and the start of your benefits. The longer the wait the lower the cost. The chart below is the cost for a $2,000/month disability income policy for a healthy non-smoking male, age thirty-five. As you can see, longer elimination periods lower cost. Remember monies in IRAs, pensions, and other qualified pension plans can be used during the elimination period without the 10% pen-

alty on premature distributions, even though you are under age 59½, if you are disabled.

ELIMINATION PERIOD

IN DAYS	COST
30	$868
60	742
90	676
180	594
365	546

Principle: Be realistic in selecting your benefit period.

As common sense would dictate, the longer the benefits run, the greater the cost of the policy. Also remember, insurance salesmen are compensated by commissions on the premiums you pay the insurance company. The higher your cost, the greater the sales commission. When your insurance salesman tells you about the twenty-one-year-old man who broke his neck and spent fifty years as a quadriplegic on the $3,000/month disability income policy, you are hearing the exception not the rule. The truth is that only approximately 10% of all disabilities last longer than one year and only 1% last longer than five years. For these reasons, I suggest you cut costs and select a short benefit period. Select a benefit period of one to five years, not to age sixty-five with a 200% to 300% greater cost. Continue to save and invest. The larger your savings the less disability income you need to buy. Eventually you can drop the insurance and rely on your savings if you are disabled.

Principle: Buy no more than the amount needed in a policy that is guaranteed renewable and noncancelable.

Insurance companies never give you an incentive for claims, so you cannot buy more than 80% of your existing pay as a benefit. If you purchase two separate policies, each for 80% of your income, so that you'll be better off disabled, you will learn that neither policy will pay more than half of the 80% maximum and you will have wasted your premiums. Insist on a policy that cannot be canceled by the company, except for non-payment of premiums, and one that is guaranteed renewable at your option. You probably will not find these two options as common in group/company plans as in individual policies, but insist on both noncancelable and guaranteed renewable contracts.

Principle: Look for policies with residual benefits.

Remember the advertising man we met who had the heart attack at age forty-eight. He elected to return to his old job part-time, eighteen months after his release from the hospital. If he had purchased a policy without residual benefits, his part-time income would have caused his disability income payments to stop. If, however, his policy provided for residual benefits at 50%, a part-time job would only reduce his disability income, not terminate the benefits.

Principle: Carefully weigh the cost and benefits of inflation adjusted benefits.

Remember insurance salesmen have a disincentive to cut costs on policies. The only way to win on a policy which has inflation adjusted benefits is to be disabled five years or longer with inflation averaging 5%/year or more. To me the cost outweighs the benefit. At best, inflation protection is a luxury not a necessity.

Principle: Purchase adequate integrated policies.

An integrated policy adjusts your monthly benefits by other outside benefits you receive. Example: A $2,000/month integrated policy would drop to $1,200/month if you received $800/month from social security. A nonintegrated policy (which costs 45% more) would continue to pay $2,000/month even though you collected $800/month from social security.

Principle: Look for rehabilitation/transition benefits.

Rehabilitation benefits would be funds you could use to equip yourself for different work. Our thoracic surgeon with three missing fingers could teach, practice general medicine, or use his transition benefit to train for another specialty like anesthesiology, dermatology, or ENT. Cost is small, but potential use is great.

Principle: For the best value at the lowest cost, shop and compare costs and benefits.

Costs vary widely from company to company. Some policies pay dividends while others pay none. If you want a competitive contract, the National Insurance Consumer Organization (NICO) suggests that you use, as a standard, a policy from the USAA Life Insurance Company (1-800-531-8000) of San Antonio, Texas. Get a price quote and a list of benefits, then shop and compare to find something better if you can. Often the best buy is a renewable disability income (RDI) policy. These policies are like term insurance. Every few years the price increases, but overall RDIs cost you less per month initially and over time.

The coverage level for the following chart is $1,000/month with a three-year term and a standard elimination period (thirty days).

AGE	LEVEL PREMIUM	RDI
30–34	$ 785	$ 396
35–39	785	464
40–44	785	620
45–49	785	880
50–54	785	1,199
TOTAL	19,625	17,795

If you total the cost of level premium disability during the twenty-five-year period the cost is $19,625. This is $1,830 more than the renewable term policy which has a total cost of $17,795. In addition, you have the power of compound interest working for you in the early years, when RDI cost is almost 50% less.

Principle: Don't waste money on return of premium.
Some companies offer an option called return of premium which enables you to receive all your premiums back at a later date (typically age sixty-five) less any benefits you have collected. The cost of this option is an increase of 50% in your premiums. If you figure the returns, you are way ahead putting the extra cost into retiring debt like credit cards, auto loans, or your home mortgage, which carry interest rates from 8% to 18%, rather than the 3% to 4% return offered on the return premium option.

Principle: Don't duplicate coverage.
Consolidate multiple policies into one policy. Take advantage of the economy of scale where rates drop for higher amounts.

Principle: Avoid hospital income policies.
The price is substantial but the benefits are limited to your time in the hospital. These days

hospital stays are getting shorter. What you want is income when you are disabled, not just while you are hospitalized.

Principle: Avoid waiver of premium and accidental death benefit.

The cost to waive premiums is substantial and the benefits are small. Buy what you need in terms of benefits, including enough to pay all your insurance premiums.

Principle: Avoid expensive "own occupational" definitions of disability.

Insurance sold to highly compensated professionals such as doctors, attorneys, executives, or media personalities stress their unique definition of disability. You are disabled if you are unable to perform the regular duties of your "own occupation" at the time of disability. A TV anchorman would be disabled if he lost his voice box due to cancer of the larynx. A surgeon who lost three fingers would be considered disabled if the policy specified "own occupation," whereas neither would generally be able to collect on either social security or their non "own occupation" disability income policies. The cost for the definition "own occupation" is 20 to 30% more in premiums. At best, this feature is a luxury, not a necessity.

To apply what you've learned, take the time now to estimate your need for disability income.

1. Take-home pay (after tax) x 75% $___ /month
2. Benefits, potential
   a. social security $___ /month
   b. workman's comp. $___ /month
   c. company/group coverage $___ /month
   d. investment income $___ /month
   e. working spouse $___ /month
   f. help from family $___ /month
   g. TOTAL personal benefits (a-f) $___ /month
3. Monthly disability income needed $___ /month
   (line 1 less line 2g)

Remember our objective is to secure adequate protection at minimal cost. To do so avoid both extremes: no protection and too much protection. Apply this information to secure adequate protection if you aren't covered or cut your cost of existing coverage 25 to 50%.

PROPERTY, CASUALTY, AND SPECIALTY COVERAGE

Priority number three is insurance on home, autos, and specialty coverage. Our goal remains adequate protection at minimal cost, avoiding the extremes of overinsuring and no coverage.

HOME INSURANCE

Basic coverage, called HO-1, is required by lenders if you have a mortgage on your home. HO-1 protects you against eleven risks, called perils: fire or lightning, windstorms or hail, explosion, riot or civil commotion, damage caused by aircraft, damage caused by vehicles, smoke, vandalism, theft, glass breakage and damage caused by that breakage, and volcanic eruption. HO-1 is basic minimal coverage. Broader coverage, HO-2, is basic coverage plus protection from six additional perils: falling objects; weight of ice, snow, or sleet; accidental discharge or overflow of water or steam from a plumbing, heating, air-conditioning, or automatic fire-protection sprinkler system, or from a household appliance; sudden and accidental tearing apart, cracking, burning, or bulging of a steam or hot water heating system, AC, or automatic fire-protection system; freezing of a plumbing, heating, AC, or automatic fire-protection sprinkler system, or of a household appliance; and sudden and accidental damage from artificially generated electric current (does not include loss to a tube, transistor, or similar electronic component). HO-2 generally costs 5 to 10% more than HO-1 and is also available for mobile homes. HO-3 or "special" homeowner's coverage protects against all seventeen perils of HO-2 plus all perils except those specifically excluded by contract, i.e., flood, earthquake, war, nuclear accident, and a few others. If you are a renter, HO-4 is comparable to HO-2. If you own a condo, coverage HO-6 is comparable to HO-2. Both exclude the dwelling itself but include personal property.

An HO-1 policy is your basic minimum coverage. For many, HO-2 is the best buy, and for a few HO-3 is worth the 10 to 15% greater cost. If you live in one of the 18,300 government specified flood-prone communities look into flood policies. Average cost is $308/year for an $85,000 dwelling. You can also buy earthquake coverage. The premiums are about 50% above regular coverage; rates vary according to the vulnerability of the house. There is also windstorm insurance available in seven coastal states vulnerable to hurricanes.

CUTTING COST ON
HOMEOWNER'S INSURANCE

First, *see if you are eligible for a discount.* Many companies offer discounts for: multiple policies (car and home insurance), smoke detectors, security systems, fire-resistant homes, nonsmokers, mature homeowners, and longtime customers. These discounts run from 2 to 20% each. *To save money ask for a discount.*

Second, since homeowner policies are sold with a deductible, *take a higher deductible to lower your cost*. A $500 deductible is approximately 10% less premium than a $250 deductible. Just as in medical, disability, car, and other insurance, the higher your deductible the lower your cost.

Third, *determine if replacement cost is worth the 10 to 15% additional premium*. There are two ways to insure personal property. An actual cash value (ACV) policy pays you what you paid for the item *minus* depreciation. A replacement policy pays you what it costs to replace the item. A sofa, for example, bought five years ago for $1,000 would lose about 50% ($500) in depreciation in five years. If fire destroys your sofa an ACV policy might pay $500 whereas a replacement cost would pay you $1,200 (today's cost to replace the same sofa).

Fourth, *determine how much protection you need for personal property*. It is worthwhile to inventory personal property by listing items, serial numbers if any, date of purchase, purchase price, and today's real value. It's a good idea to photograph or videotape these items as well and keep the list, photo, or tape along with any appraisals in a safe place. Most policies cover personal property up to 50% of the value of your home. For a higher cost you can increase that protection. For some items there is a limit for theft that varies with individual items. Remember most personal property declines in value over time. Personal property in estate sales is often sold at 15 to 20% of the original purchase price. *Don't overinsure.*

Fifth, *evaluate the cost to schedule and insure specific items.* Most policies have floating coverage for personal property that "floats" with the property wherever it goes. Floaters cover jewelry, furs, cameras, computers, musical instruments, silverware, china, crystal, stamps, coins, paintings, and other valuables. Since personal property is covered in a standard schedule with set policy limits for each category, you should compare your inventory and estimate of today's value to your policies' limits. Sometimes your best buy is to increase the standard limit from $1,000 to $5,000 on jewelry, for example, rather than purchase a special policy to cover an expensive piece of jewelry. Before you decide, ask for the price. Special floaters or specifically scheduled items can cost up to 15% of the price of the item per year.

Sixth, *determine how much liability you need.* Your policy offers liability protection for bodily injury or property damage caused by you, a family member, or a pet. It protects you from the claim for damages, including the cost of defending yourself if you are sued, not only at home but elsewhere in the U.S. and Canada. Most policies provide $100,000 in liability coverage. For $10/year more you can raise the limit to $300,000. If you have a high net worth you may want to *consider buying an "umbrella" policy* that extends your liability coverage to $1 million or more. Umbrella policies pick up where your home and car insurance liability stops. They cost from $150 to $200 a year for $1 million in coverage. It is generally cheaper to buy a separate umbrella for one-half million or more than to raise the liability limits on your home and car to $500,000.

Seventh, as with all insurance, *shop and compare policies*. A good source of information is *Consumer Reports*, a monthly publication of Consumer Union, available by subscription or in your local library.

Eighth, *make sure you have been accurate on the price of your home* to avoid overpaying or loss of protection. If your home is worth $100,000, part of the price, perhaps $20,000, is attributable to the price of the land. Since the price of the home insurance varies directly with the price of the home, don't pay for 25% more coverage than you need by insuring a $20,000 lot and paying for a $100,000 policy.

The flip side is always: Have your home insured for what it would cost to replace it, if possible. If your home, not including land value, is insured for less than 80–90% of its value, depending on your policy, you will not collect in full on a loss. In some areas of the country, homes have declined in value but the costs to replace a home have continued to rise. In other areas, homes have risen dramatically in price, and most homeowners have not increased the values for which their homes are insured. Reevaluate your home insurance each year to avoid overpaying or underprotecting.

Ninth, if possible *eliminate the extra ½% per year you pay on your mortgage if your loan is greater than 80% of the value of your home.* Lenders can and do require a premium of ½% if the equity in your home is less than 20%. If your equity is or can be increased above 20% you can save a bundle. For example, a $100,000 loan at 8% interest for thirty years costs you 360 payments of $740/month with total interest payments of $166,482. If you take away the ½% interest by having 20% equity or more, you find a $100,000 loan at 7½% interest for thirty years gives payments of $706/month with total interest of $154,014. This saves you $34/month or $416/year, and $12,468 in interest for a thirty-year loan.

Tenth and final, *do not buy homeowner's insurance, mortgage life insurance, or mortgage disability payment insurance from a lender* for three reasons. First, you will pay several times what you could purchase the same policy for separately if you shopped and compared. Despite the belief that all policies cost about the same, prices vary up to 400% for the same policy. Insurance is not federally regulated but regulated individually by fifty separate states and state departments. Second, you can save money by buying in volume. It is much cheaper to buy one $100,000 policy than ten $10,000 policies. Finally, insurance should be purchased by considering your overall needs and plans, not just one area such as your home, autos, or loans.

If you will invest the time to study each area of insurance until you understand it and are able to quantify and qualify your needs, you will be able to shop and compare policies, saving yourself hundreds of dollars each year in unnecessary costs. By applying the information covered so far you will probably save yourself more than $1,000/year.

Now let's examine an expensive, little understood area of property and casualty coverage:

AUTO INSURANCE

Auto insurance can be broken into three components: liability, collision, and comprehensive coverage. Let's begin by examining liability's two parts: bodily injury and property damage. Coverage is usually quoted by three numbers separated by a slash, e.g., 10/30/20. Each number represents benefits in thousands. Thus, 10/30/20 means your liability is $*10*,000 per person liability coverage (for bodily injury) up to a maximum benefit of $*30*,000 for the accident, with a maximum property damage of $*20*,000. If you hit a Mercedes carrying six people, the maximum your policy would pay toward occupants' injuries would be $30,000 divided by six people or $5,000 each. The most your policy would pay toward repairing or replacing the Mercedes would be $20,000. *You are liable and responsible for damages above those limits.*

Today scores of personal injury lawyers are advertising for clients on TV, on radio, and in newspapers. As I write this a national pizza chain has suspended its offer of free pizza if it takes longer than thirty minutes for you to get delivery of your order. The thirty-minute-or-less guarantee was suspended because of an $84 million settlement to the estate of a woman killed in an auto accident involving a driver for the pizza maker. A recent newspaper story told of a man who sued a city's subway system for $7 million and won. In a drunken state, he fell off the platform and lost both legs to an approaching train. Do you remember the multimillion dollar settlement against an airplane manufacturing company for a plane built thirty years prior that crashed and killed the pilot? With only 4% of the world population, the U.S.A. accounts for 95% of the world's litigation! The system desperately needs reform.

The next time you visit your doctor ask him or her what malpractice insurance costs. If you knew the number of patients he or she sees each year you could easily calculate how much more that costs you per office visit. The same is true for all insurance, including your auto liability. In the last ten years 450,000 people died in auto accidents. Many of the deaths resulted in lawsuits with settlements ranging from $10,000 to $84 million. Guess who pays for the settlements? You the consumer, in higher prices for goods and services, including your own insurance. The odds of being killed in an auto accident or killing someone else are 1.5 out of 100 this year! That is 20 times the odds of being killed on a train, 40 times the odds of dying in a plane, 200 times the odds of being killed by lightning, 4,000 times the odds of contracting cancer from exposure to carcinogens from factories, and 24,000 times the odds of winning the Arizona lottery. *Protect yourself against the possibility of a lawsuit if you have anything to lose.*

Different states have different rules and amounts of required coverage. The minimum required coverage in Arizona is 10/30/10. In Arizona you can't register your car without proving you have the minimum required liability coverage. (That law is currently being appealed despite the drop in accidents.) Still today, 20% of the drivers in my home state drive with no insurance. How much liability coverage do you need? The greater of: (a) your state's required minimum or (b) your net worth plus potential legal fees. Net worth is what you own (assets) less what you owe (liabilities). The more you have, the greater is your need to protect your assets. I suggest minimum coverage from $25,000 to

$100,000 per person and $50,000 to $250,000 per occurrence. If your net worth exceeds $100,000, look into adding a separate umbrella policy. It is less costly than increasing your existing liability coverage within your policy.

Minimum coverage for property damage should be $25,000 to $50,000. Adequate coverage would be $50,000 to $100,000. To find out what your current coverage is find the "Declarations" page for your auto policy, and compare what you have with what is required and/or necessary. *Buy minimum coverage from 25/100/25 to 100/200/50 or your state's minimum, whichever is greater.* I have seen people reduce their liability coverage, add a $1 million umbrella, and cut costs by buying no more coverage than necessary.

AUTO COLLISION COVERAGE

Collision coverage pays for the cost to repair your vehicle, whereas liability covers the other party. A simple but very effective way to cut cost is to raise your deductible. Deductibles can be zero, $50, $100, $150, $200, $250, $500, or $1,000. By selecting a higher deductible you can reduce the cost of collision from 10 to 50%. If your car is older, you may consider dropping collision insurance totally. Caution: When you raise deductibles or cancel coverage you are responsible for the deductible or loss.

Consider saving rather than spending your savings. The odds of being involved in a car wreck reported to the police (in Phoenix, Arizona) are one in seven each calendar year. Remember, "The wise man saves some of his paycheck but the fool spends whatever he [or she] gets" (Proverbs 21:20 LB). If you save the reduction in premiums, you will be glad you did.

Comprehensive coverage pays for the cost of repairing your vehicle for non-collision causes like fire, theft, and vandalism. Again select higher deductibles to lower the cost, and consider dropping coverage when the value of your car reaches a pre-determined point. Specialty coverage for items like sophisticated, expensive car stereo systems, special tires and wheels, and antique or collectible cars is very expensive and generally not worth the price.

Before we consider a number of additional money saving ideas, let's consider insurance on a special high risk category of drivers—*teenagers.* Teenage males are twice as expensive to insure as females because insurance company statistics show the highest risk class for drivers to be males age sixteen to twenty-one. Some companies go up to age twenty-four, whereas others offer breaks for students and young marrieds. Let me illustrate with my oldest son who went from an occasional driver of my four-year-old Honda Civic ($800/year premium cost) to the primary driver of a four-year-old Geo ($1,600/year premium). The Geo cost $4,100, but his insurance, which was bought with $1,000 deductibles for collision and comprehensive and 25/100/25 liability, cost 39% of the price of the car! That was before his speeding ticket and an accident which was his fault. With two citations his premium jumped to $3,360/year ($280/month). He was forced to sell his car and return to public transportation, friends, and family for rides. Today, three years later, he is driving a seven-year-old car and pays his own insurance of $1,800/year from his part-time, after school job. If you have or will have teenage drivers, here are a few guidelines to help you and your growing young adults:

(1) seek good student discounts;

(2) have your teenagers take driver's education *and* defensive driving;

(3) save money while they are away from home at college;

(4) decide up-front, in writing, who pays for insurance, how tickets and accidents will be handled, and what and how rules will be enforced;

(5) consider a truck rather than a car—trucks are cheaper to insure;

(6) notice that type of car determines insurance cost—check before buying and avoid sports/performance cars, e.g., Corvettes, Firebirds, 300Zs, etc.;

(7) purchase an eight- to ten-year-old car in good mechanical condition;

(8) stress the necessity of defensive, safe driving and teenage driving statistics;

(9) realize cars are a luxury, not a necessity; cars/trucks carry personal and financial responsibility—that's the price for privilege;

(10) if possible qualify for multiple car discounts.

SAVE ON INSURANCE

You can *save significantly by pursuing and/or qualifying for discounts*. Many of the ten tips listed above for teenagers will work for you. In addition to discounts for females age 30–64 ask for discounts for:

(1) air bags;

(2) anti lock braking systems (ABS);

(3) antitheft systems (mine cost $25);

(4) nonsmokers;

(5) nondrinkers;

(6) senior citizens;

(7) farmers;

(8) multiple policies and longtime policy holder discounts.

Each of these eight ideas can decrease policy cost from 5 to 20%.

Avoid the following coverages unless they are required by law in your state:

(1) no fault or PIP coverage.

(2) accidental death benefit and loss of sight.

(3) road service/towing—especially if you have an automobile club like AAA.

(4) car rental and insurance on rental cars— use a credit card to pay that pays the insurance on a rental car.

When you rent a car for business or personal reasons, charge the car to your Gold Visa card. Visa pays the costs to the car rental company if you are involved in an accident. Check with your credit card issuer to get the same benefit. If you figure out the cost of insurance on a rental car you will find that the major rental companies are 300 to 500% higher than your existing car insurance policy. You may even be covered on your existing auto insurance— read your policy carefully to find out.

(5) medical payments—covered by your medical policy.

(6) uninsured and underinsured motorists; the coverage benefits your company not you.

(7) credit life, disability, and car insurance on your auto loan; buy them separately and in volume.

Avoiding these options will cut your cost without significantly increasing your risk.

Here are some additional ways to save money on auto insurance: *Don't file claims for less than $500;* claims will usually raise your insurance costs for the next three years. To be certain check with your company. *Find out what an accident or ticket will do to your cost*, then you will have motivation to drive safely and defensively. *Explore part-time coverage*, generally six months or less, for seasonal items like snowmobiles, golf carts, motorcycles, and mopeds. Finally, as in all areas, *study to learn what you need, then shop and compare* policies and prices. My assistant, Candy Harris, did her homework, decided what she needed, then shopped and compared. She saved herself and her husband $1,200 per year in car insurance premiums.

SPECIALTY COVERAGE

Extended warranties on new vehicles and *service contracts* or agreements on everything you buy are generally a waste of money. Since warranties and service contracts pay high commissions to the salesman (30–70% of the premium), more and more retailers and merchants offer you their contracts. Auto extended warranties, for example, pay out approximately 15% of premiums collected in claims. For every story they tell you about the consumer who got a new engine a year after the factory warranty expired, there are thirty or more who paid for but never used their extended warranty. I have a security-conscious friend who spent $1,800 over the last three years buying almost every warranty, contract, and agreement he was offered. His big screen TV, VCR, camcorder, stereo, and truck are all protected. As of today, he has not collected a penny in benefits. Save your money. Do your own repairs out of your savings. You will come out way ahead 85% of the time.

FINANCIAL CONTRACTS

Besides warranties and service agreements, if you finance a purchase you will probably be offered credit life and disability. Most retailers of major items—furniture, refrigerators, washers/dryers, cars, and trucks—offer you life insurance that pays off your loan if you or your spouse dies. This is very high priced decreasing term insurance. If you need insurance, read on and learn where, when, and how to buy. *Don't buy life insurance "convenient" from lenders;* it's 200 to 500% more money. The same recommendation holds for payment protection or disability income which makes loan payments for you, generally after six months, and only if you are permanently and totally disabled. Buy disability income from your group at work or from an agent, not from a lender. You get two to six times more protection at the same cost. If you feel you must buy extended warranties, despite my advice, don't finance the warranty at 10 to 20% interest in your contract. If you can't wait to drive home that new or used car or truck, don't finance one year of car insurance in a five-year payment plan. If you do, get ready for a surprise in years two, three, four, and five when you get to buy insurance separately and in addition to your regular payments.

TRAVEL POLICIES

I have tried to learn the amount of money collected by policies that pay if you are killed or maimed while traveling on a plane, bus, or train, but the information is not available. I do know the cost per dollar of benefit is five to ten times what you could buy if you bought a separate policy through an agent. Today you can buy trip cancellation insurance, luggage insurance, and everything except insurance against bad weather. Save your money.

BURIAL POLICIES

I was shocked to find that 80 percent of my retired clients still have burial policies on their lives to pay for final costs. Almost without exception they repositioned these cash values after they read the following section on life insurance. Those policies were written many years ago. Since then the cost of insurance has declined to a fraction of what it was. If you own a burial policy read the section on life insurance.

It does make good sense to *pre-plan your burial and funeral arrangements*. This will eliminate the tendencies loved ones have to splurge and overspend on funerals to demonstrate how much the departed ones meant to them. A good plan to reduce burial costs is called the Memorial Society. This plan guarantees that at your death all burial costs will be provided at a low cost. The plan is offered through most funeral homes, or you can get more information by contacting:

> Continental Association of Funeral
> and Memorial Society
> 6900 Lost Lake Road
> Egg Harbor, WI 54209
> Phone 1-800-458-5563

You can go to the funeral home in advance and prepay the final costs. When or if you do, negotiate for a lower cost. The families of those who do not plan end up paying 40 to 200% more. For those frugal souls out there like me (others call us cheap), you might consider donating your body to a medical school. The school will use your body for experiments or training young doctors and in turn will provide burial at no cost.

NURSING HOME POLICIES

With life spans extending longer and longer, many people now consider nursing home insurance for their later years so they will not be a burden to family and loved ones. Two free booklets you should obtain, read, and study:

Guide to Long-Term Care Insurance
American Association of Retired People
1909 K Street, NW
ACLI Publications Request Dept.
Washington, D.C. 20049

Consumer Guide to Long Term Care
Health Insurance Association of America
1001 Pennsylvania Ave., NW
Washington, D.C. 20004

To save money *don't buy coverage early,* prior to retirement. Granted it is 50 to 70% cheaper at age fifty-five, but compare that to saving what you would have spent for ten years including interest. Compounded savings could build you a sizable nest egg which could be used to pay a nursing home or reduce the cost of a nursing home policy. In calculating necessary benefits, remember available sources of income like pensions, social security, and investment income so you *buy only the amount you need.* Most policies have a twenty-day to one-year elimination period, a specified monthly or daily benefit amount, and benefit periods that continue from one to five years. The Nursing Home Industry tells us the average stay in a nursing home is less than ninety days. Since less than 5% require more than three years, look at benefit periods of twelve to thirty-six months for the best value. You might want to *consider inflation adjusted benefits* since during the last decade we have seen prices for nursing homes rise at 250% of CPI. You will also want to determine whether you will need "custodial," "intermediate," or "skilled care" benefits. From my experience, the better solution is home care/custodial benefits which cost far less than skilled care and seem to be more acceptable and preferred most by patients themselves.

Good nursing home coverage is not cheap. A survey of seven top rated, safe companies offering policies for: a seventy-year-old male, $80/day benefit, beginning in thirty days, lasting for three years, with inflation adjusted benefits costs from $1,200 to $1,800/year. If you selected a six-month delay the costs drop 50%. Even then for a retiree on a fixed income the price is not cheap.

There are other options you should consider prior to purchasing a policy. If you have limited assets, there is the safety net of Medicaid. In addition, many churches offer care in church-owned homes in return for assignment of pension and social security benefits regardless of the amount. For those with spouses, I recommend securing advice from qualified attorneys, financial or estate planners, or advisers familiar with problems of the retired. There is nothing wrong with spending principal to provide for your later years. You accumulated capital so that you wouldn't be a burden. Use that capital and earnings to pay for the cost if it becomes necessary. If it's not necessary, I encourage you to create a solid estate plan that covers all the bases. My book *Saving the Best for Last* (Moody, 1994) deals with estate planning.

LIFE INSURANCE

Now, your favorite topic—life insurance, priority #4. The first step is determining how much you need.

Ask your agent and you will hear "much more than you have" or "that depends on how long you are going to be dead." Most consumers have little love and less tolerance for insurance men who provide little information and lots of pressure. Consumers are wary of the zeal and enthusiasm with which salesmen approach their products. Just as in every profession, there are professional, knowledgeable, client-centered advisers, and there are high pressure, under-educated pitch men out to make a fast buck. Why do you get so many answers to the simple question, "How much life insurance do I need?"

One answer is that each of us is unique with different circumstances. How many children do you have? What are their ages? Do you have other dependents? What are their personal and financial circumstances? Are you married? What are your spouse's earning capacity and desires? Are you divorced? Are you a single parent? What do I need to know about your spouse? Is yours a first, second, or later marriage? How large are your debts, loans, mortgages, and liabilities? What kind of lifestyle do you want to provide those you leave behind? What is your net worth? How large is your investment and passive income? What is the nature and type of your assets? What education do you want to provide for your dependents? What will that cost? How much do you need, want, or desire to leave your heirs? Do you want to factor inflation into your plans? What are your goals? If you answered these twenty questions and provided the data to ten different professional agents they would come surprisingly close to answering the question of how much insurance you need.

To simplify let's look at four groups. First is a group with little or no need for life insurance: singles, children, students, and those without dependents. Second, those with possible needs for life insurance: the rich, retired, non-working spouses, DINKS (dual income, no kids), and OINKS (one income, no kids). Third, the probable: singles with dependents. Finally, the definite: business owners, professionals, and families with dependents (children or adults). The goal of insurance is to *provide* for family and dependents, not to *protect* them from reliance and dependence on God. "Trust in the Lord with all your heart, and do not lean on your own understanding. In all your ways acknowledge Him, and He will make your paths straight" (Proverbs 3:5–6).

The purpose of life insurance is to replace part or all of the income of a person who dies. You can provide assets through insurance, which will provide investment income. Think of life insurance as buying time for you to accumulate assets which will provide assets and income to your loved ones if you die. A rule of thumb is to purchase five to ten times your gross income, but that does not consider your answers to the twenty questions asked earlier. Another question you need to answer is what would the money earn that insurance provided. If CDs earn 3%, government bonds earn 6%, and investments earn 10%, you would get three different answers to how much income would be provided by a $500,000 policy: $15,000/year, $30,000/year, or $50,000/year. How knowledgeable and experienced is your beneficiary at investing and managing assets? How much risk do you want him or her to take? Is spending principal a good decision? What rate of inflation do you want to factor into your plans? How much control are you willing to give your beneficiary? What about your spouse remarrying? Not easy or simple answers, are they?

Let me ask a few more questions you need to answer, then we will look at a guideline based on income. Are there existing debts (credit cards, auto loans, personal loans, and mortgages) that should be paid off? Should a surviving spouse work? Starting when? For how long? What assets do you have that could or should be repositioned to generate income? What social security benefits would your beneficiaries receive? For how long? What about the period between the time when benefits stop and when a spouse becomes eligible to receive social security retirement benefits? What personal and charitable benefits do you want to provide? After you have completed my easy insurance planner on page 60, ask God to give you wisdom and discernment to arrive at your own answer.

If you will take the time to work through this calculation you will quickly see that the entry on each line will be different for each individual and family. Do this planner for yourself to see how much life insurance you need. Then use the same process to estimate your needs for retirement. That will motivate you toward learning more about good stewardship and will increase your desire to save, plan, and eliminate unnecessary costs from your spending plan.

Once you arrive at your needs for insurance, review your needs annually and at major events like births, deaths, marriages, graduations, new homes,

EASY INSURANCE PLANNER (example)

1. Family's Necessary Cost of Living: $50,000/year

2. Family's Annual Income from:

Social security	$12,000
Spouse's earnings	20,000
Investment income (6% pretax)	3,000
Other income	3,000
TOTAL	38,000

3. Family Income Deficit   12,000/year

4. Filling the Gap
   Spouse's life expectancy (see appendix) 40 years
   Estimated investment income (see appendix) 6%
   How long will money last (see appendix)   at 4%
      divide line 3 by annual
      percentage withdrawal to find
   Additional assets needed $300,000

5. Debt Retirement   5,000

6. College Educational Fund for Children   50,000

7. Other Amounts/Bequests   5,000

8. Total Life Insurance Needed $360,000
   (lines 4, 5, 6, & 7)

EASY INSURANCE PLANNER

1. Family's Necessary Cost of Living: $ _____ /year

2. Family's Annual Income from:
   Social security $ _____
   Spouse's earnings   _____
   Investment income (6% pretax)   _____
   Other income   _____
   TOTAL   _____

3. Family Income Deficit   _____ /year

4. Filling the Gap
   Spouse's life expectancy (see appendix) __ years
   Estimated investment income (see appendix) __%
   How long will money last (see appendix) at __%
      divide line 3 by annual
      percentage withdrawal to find
   Additional assets needed $ _____

5. Debt Retirement   _____

6. College Educational Fund for Children   _____

7. Other Amounts/Bequests   _____

8. Total Life Insurance Needed $ _____
   (lines 4, 5, 6, & 7)

major purchases, and major loans (especially business or investment loans).

TYPES OF COVERAGE

If your goal is maximum coverage at minimum cost, the answer is: Buy term insurance. There are two major categories of life insurance—with and without cash values. It is my recommendation that you do not consider cash value/surrender benefit type policies until:

(1) you are completely free of credit card debt;

(2) you are saving to buy cars in cash rather than over time;

(3) you have a spending plan with a positive surplus;

(4) you have adequate savings of at least six months' living expenses;

(5) you have your home paid for—no mortgages or loans.

Read my first book, *Dollars & Sense* (NavPress, 1993) for more details and explanations.

Traditional life insurance salesmen will attempt to convince you to buy cash value coverage called whole life, limited pay, and endowment contracts. Let's listen in on a typical insurance sales presentation to a male age thirty-five. "You can buy a $100,000 non-participating term policy to age sixty-five for only $750 per year." That sounds OK to you, but before you say anything, I add, "But your insurance will be all gone at age sixty-five and you don't want that, do you?" You think you wouldn't want that to happen, so you say no. If you analyzed the question, by age sixty-five you should have money saved. But without allowing you to analyze what I say, I continue. "Here's a policy for only $1,500/year that never runs out. It's called *whole life.* Permanent protection, not insurance that expires just as you approach your later years where the odds of dying really start to increase." I fail to tell you that the premiums continue to age one hundred! Before you can speak, here I come again. "You don't want to pay premiums all your life, do you? Here's a policy for $2,500 per year that you can quit paying on in twenty years. It's all paid up. We call it *20 pay life.*" Notice the increasing cost, and remember I am paid a percentage of your premiums. The higher the cost the larger my commission. "Let me tell you what I would buy if I were you—an *endowment contract.* At the end of twenty years you have paid in $80,000 but your contract is worth $100,000. You've had free insurance for twenty years and made a $20,000 profit. Isn't that amazing? Which policy do you think is best—the 20 pay or the endowment?"

Examine exactly what is being offered by looking at where you would be with each of these four policies if you died ten years after you had purchased it. In each case, your heirs or beneficiary would collect $100,000. The term buyer's outlay was $7,500; the whole life buyer spent $15,000; the 20 pay policy cost $25,000; and the endowment buyer spent $40,000. If your objective is adequate protection at minimal cost, buy *term insurance* and put the difference in cost into retiring debt with interest rates of 8 to 18% like credit cards, cars, and home mortgages.

But what if you live beyond age sixty-five, when your term insurance expires? Let's assume you are a non-smoking female, age thirty-five, and you purchase term insurance at the maximum rate given on page 67 of this booklet. You have compared the price of term insurance with that of whole life (in this example, from Massachusetts Savings Bank Life, #1 rated whole life in *Consumer Reports*, September 1993, with a premium of $1,098/year to age one hundred), so you decide to invest the difference between term and whole life insurance. Let's look at how much you will have invested by age sixty-five. The following chart assumes that the difference in price between policies is invested at the beginning of each year at 10%. As you accumulate savings, you cut down on the amount of term insurance purchased (column 4), but the amount of your savings and insurance added together always total at least $100,000 (column 5).

AGE	COST OF TERM	SAVINGS	AMOUNT OF TERM	DEATH BENEFIT (INSURANCE PLUS SAVINGS)
35	$74	$1,126	$100,000	$101,126
36	78	2,361	100,000	102,361
37	82	3,715	100,000	103,715
38	86	5,199	100,000	105,199
39	90	6,828	100,000	106,828
40	95	8,614	100,000	108,614
41	92	10,582	92,000	102,582
42	94	12,744	90,000	102,744
43	96	15,121	87,000	102,121
44	97	17,734	85,000	102,734
45	98	20,607	82,000	102,607
46	101	23,777	79,000	102,777
47	105	27,247	75,000	102,247
48	110	31,059	72,000	103,059
49	111	35,251	67,000	102,251
50	110	39,862	63,000	102,862
51	108	44,937	57,000	101,937
52	107	50,521	52,000	102,521
53	102	56,669	46,000	102,669
54	91	63,444	38,000	101,444
55	78	70,910	30,000	100,910
56	61	79,141	22,000	101,141
57	39	88,220	13,000	101,220
58	8	98,241	3,000	101,241
59	0	109,270	-0-	109,270
60	0	121,404	-0-	121,404
61	0	134,753	-0-	134,753
62	0	149,436	-0-	149,436
63	0	165,589	-0-	165,589
64	0	183,353	-0-	183,353
65	0	202,897	-0-	202,897

You may encounter a high-tech type of cash value policy under the names Interest Sensitive Life, Universal life, Variable Life, Single Pay Life, Second to Die Life, Living Benefit policies, and more. These more recent products can be less costly than traditional cash value insurance and are often accompanied by computer-generated illustrations and proposals no layman could possibly evaluate. Most of these illustrations come with very sophisticated methods to evaluate and compare costs: interest adjusted cost, net payment index, or surrender cost index. As you have heard or seen, numbers can be crunched to prove whatever you wish them to prove. To help you fend off higher cost, higher tech salespeople use the following chart from the National Insurance Consumer Organization (NICO) of the maximum you should pay for term insurance per $1,000 of coverage per year. These rates are for a $100,000 policy. Smaller policies are slightly more. Rates do not include a policy fee of $0 to $60. If you want more information, order NICO's guide *Taking the Bite Out of Insurance*. In addition, price quotes for term insurance can be obtained from:

Insurance Information Inc.   1-800-472-5800
Select Quote of San Francisco   1-800-343-1985
Term Quote of Dayton, Ohio   1-800-444-TERM (8376)
Financial Independence Group   1-800-527-1155
NICO, 121 N. Payne St., Alexandria, VA 22314

THE MOST YOU SHOULD
PAY FOR TERM INSURANCE

NONSMOKERS ANNUAL PREMIUM			SMOKERS ANNUAL PREMIUM		
AGE	MALE	FEMALE	AGE	MALE	FEMALE
18–30	$ .76	$ .68	18–30	$1.05	$1.01
31	.76	.69	31	1.10	1.05
32	.77	.70	32	1.15	1.10
33	.78	.71	33	1.21	1.15
34	.79	.72	34	1.28	1.20
35	.80	.74	35	1.35	1.25
36	.84	.78	36	1.45	1.31
37	.88	.82	37	1.56	1.38
38	.92	.86	38	1.68	1.45
39	.97	.90	39	1.81	1.52
40	1.03	.95	40	1.95	1.60
41	1.09	1.00	41	2.12	1.73
42	1.17	1.05	42	2.30	1.89
43	1.25	1.10	43	2.50	2.05
44	1.34	1.15	44	2.72	2.22
45	1.45	1.20	45	2.95	2.40
46	1.59	1.29	46	3.22	2.59
47	1.74	1.41	47	3.52	2.79
48	1.91	1.53	48	3.85	3.01
49	2.10	1.66	49	4.21	3.23
50	2.30	1.76	50	4.60	3.50
51	2.49	1.90	51	4.97	3.79
52	2.70	2.06	52	5.38	4.10
53	2.96	2.22	53	5.82	4.44
54	3.40	2.40	54	6.29	4.80
55	3.40	2.60	55	6.80	5.20
56	3.66	2.79	56	7.31	5.58
57	3.94	3.00	57	7.87	5.99

	NONSMOKERS ANNUAL PREMIUM			SMOKERS ANNUAL PREMIUM	
AGE	MALE	FEMALE	AGE	MALE	FEMALE
58	$4.23	$3.22	58	$ 8.46	$ 6.43
59	4.55	3.46	59	9.10	6.90
60	4.90	3.70	60	9.80	7.40
61	5.43	3.98	61	10.83	7.95
62	6.02	4.28	62	11.98	8.54
63	6.67	4.60	63	13.25	9.18
64	7.40	4.93	64	14.65	9.86
65	8.20	5.30	65	16.20	10.60

Some agents approach you today with the phrase "buy term and invest the difference." They offer you term insurance plus either mutual funds or an array of insurance products: single or flexible premium deferred annuities, fixed or variable premium variable annuities, fixed or variable immediate annuities, split annuities, and more. Two suggestions will help you. First, compare the cost of term insurance to the above chart. Second, concentrate on retiring all debt prior to investing. Paying off an 8% guaranteed mortgage is wiser than gambling that you might make more by investing.

BEWARE OF MYTHS

Too much expensive cash value insurance is sold with myths that sound believable. Let's examine some of the most common:

MYTH: Insurance will never cost less than it does today. Buy it now!
TRUTH: All insurance is based on "mortality tables" which are revised over time. The cost of insurance declined from 1940 to 1980. If your policy is based on a pre-1980 mortality table, you are overpaying for your protection. Insurance may get cheaper.

MYTH: Participating policies (mutual companies) are cheaper than non-participating policies (stock companies).
TRUTH: The so-called dividends issued by mutual companies are not true dividends but rebates on overcharge of premium without interest. That's why they are not taxable (Treasury decision 1743).

MYTH: All companies charge about the same price.
TRUTH: Rates are not regulated. Companies charge what the traffic will bear. Rates vary up to 400% for the same policy.

MYTH: It is cheaper when you're young. Buy insurance on your children now to guarantee their future insurability.
TRUTH: Buy insurance only when you have a need, like when you have dependents.

MYTH: A paid-up policy costs you nothing and continues to grow in value.

TRUTH: A paid-up policy earns 3 to 4% per year, part of which pays the cost of your "free insurance." Meanwhile you pay 8 to 10% on credit cards, car loans, and mortgages. A paid-up policy is a great deal for the insurance company, not for you.

MYTH: The cash values in your policies are "your savings."
TRUTH: If you take your savings, you lose your insurance. If you die, the company keeps your savings. If you need money, it costs 4 to 8% interest to borrow "your own money." Why would you pay interest to use your money? Imagine a bank that charged you interest to withdraw money from your checking or savings account. Would you bank there? Then don't bank with a cash value contract.

MYTH: Cash value loans are a good, cheap way to borrow money.
TRUTH: Replace the policy with a term policy at less than one-half the price, and pay for whatever you want with no interest at all.

MYTH: You always need insurance.
TRUTH: By retirement you either have money saved, in which case you need no insurance; or you don't, in which case the last thing you need is overpriced insurance premiums.

MYTH: Buy insurance in your retirement plan with deductible premiums.

TRUTH: Ask your accountant about PS58 rates for imputed income, designed to discourage you from buying insurance in a qualified retirement plan, which is fully taxable at ordinary rates on your form 1040.

MYTH: Our policy has vanishing premiums. Only make seven to ten payments and the policy pays for itself.

TRUTH: Is that guaranteed or estimated? I call these **PACMAN** policies which devour your cash values. Use the cash value to pay off high interest debt. Buy term insurance for lowest cost.

MYTH: For best value, mix permanent insurance and term together.

TRUTH: Eliminate the permanent (cash value) and lower your cost.

MYTH: Pure term is a waste of money; you have nothing to show for it.

TRUTH: How about "protection over time." Try that line on your medical insurance, home insurance, or car insurance. Those are term policies.

MYTH: Cash value is like owning; term is like renting.

TRUTH: The real difference is the agent's commission obtained by manipulating you to overpay for insurance coverage.

MYTH: Term gets too expensive later on.
TRUTH: So do all types of life insurance. Start saving now. I have never yet met anyone who retired on his or her cash values alone.

MYTH: Insurance is a good investment.
TRUTH: Insurance is a fair investment at best. You have to hold the policy twenty years before you earn a profit in many policies.

MYTH: Insurance is a good way to save. It's like forced savings.
TRUTH: If you ever calculate the price you will reconsider.

MYTH: Insurance is a tax advantaged saving and/ or investment account.
TRUTH: An IRA or 401K is too, and here the entire cost is tax-deductible within limits.

WHAT TO BUY

Now that I have alienated most cash value life insurance salesmen, let's examine what type of terms to purchase. Begin with a company that is well-rated by all five major rating agencies (see page 20). Purchase a contract that is guaranteed renewable at your option. Look for non-smoker, preferred categories. If you are a smoker, stop. You will save thousands over your working years. To see how much you will save refer back to pages 67–68. If you can't afford the amount of term insurance you need, buy what you can afford.

There are three basic types of term life insurance:

Annual Renewable Term (ART)
Decreasing Term (DT)
Level Term (LT)

ART has a fixed amount of coverage, and each year the premium increases. You can buy ART up to age ninety or one hundred. Companies offer two quotes: a guaranteed rate and a current rate. The current rate is lower than the guaranteed rate, but the company retains the right to charge you the higher guaranteed rate if they experience adverse claims or poor investment performance in the future. Some ART is "set back" or "reentry" term (RET). Your rate can be reduced if you agree to take a physical examination in the future to prove you are still healthy. If you don't take the exam or fail it, you still have coverage at their guaranteed rates. Most company-offered life insurance is group ART. Group coverage is almost always a good buy.

Decreasing term is the reverse of ART. DT has a fixed price, but each year your amount of insurance coverage decreases. DT is offered with either level declining coverage over five to one hundred years, or decreasing coverage matching the principal pay down of an amortized loan like your home mortgage. Either type offers less coverage in the future. Straight line coverage drops the same amount each year while mortgage insurance drops less in early years and more in later years. DT is generally not wise because it is overpriced initially, and you do not have the choice of deciding whether your insurance should decline. With either LT or ART, premiums are less and you have a choice.

LT is level coverage for a fixed time period. LT is available for five, ten, fifteen, or twenty years, or to age sixty-five. Many times a level term is the sum of ART premiums averaged over the time period. In a ten-year LT policy, you overpay the first five years then underpay the next five years. At the end of the selected period your coverage remains the same, but the cost increases significantly. Some buyers dislike ART since every year the cost increases. They prefer policies that go up every five or ten years (LT). For others the reverse is true.

To see the possibilities, examine the following illustration for a male age thirty-five with a $100,000 policy:

AGE	ART	RET	5 YR (LT)	10 YR (LT)	20 YR (LT)
35	$99	$130	$115	$145	$220
36	152	143	"	"	"
37	174	156	"	"	"
38	187	169	"	"	"
39	202	182	"	"	"
40	222	149	175	"	"
41	244	175	"	"	"
42	268	205	"	"	"
43	295	237	"	"	"
44	326	290	"	"	"
45	368	200	220	250	"
46	394	208	"	"	"
47	422	215	"	"	"
48	452	255	"	"	"
49	484	305	"	"	"
50	520	205	310	"	"
51	562	260	"	"	"
52	610	321	"	"	"
53	667	388	"	"	"
54	731	462	"	"	"
TOTALS	$7,739	$4,647	$4,100	$3,950	$4,400

Each column's rates are selected from Good National. Which do you think is the cheapest? If you look at the total premiums paid for the twenty-year period the best buys in order are ten-year LT, five-year LT, twenty-year LT, RET, and ART. If you died during the first year your best buys in order are ART, five-year LT, RET, ten-year LT, with twenty-year LT last. The answer to which is best depends on how long you need to keep the coverage and what you do with the difference in premiums saved. For most planning, I recommend a one- to five-year time period; premiums are generally lowest with RET, five-year LT, or ART.

Unfortunately, most insurance agents do not recommend term insurance. They recommend cash value products. The following story will illustrate why. Agent Dan sells only term insurance policies with a $250,000 death benefit for an annual premium of $300. Each day he sells a policy. At the end of the year he has sold term policies to 250 families. He has sold $62.5 million of term insurance with total premiums of $75,000. His commissions are $48,750.

Dan's best friend Dave sells only cash value policies with a $100,000 death benefit for a cost of $1,000 per year. Just like Dan, Dave sells a policy each day. At the end of the year Dave has sold $25 million in coverage (40% of Dan's) with total annual premiums of $250,000 (250% of Dan's), but Dave earned commissions of $212,500 (436% of Dan's). If you were selling insurance would you model Dan or Dave?

The insurance company, its products, and its salesmen are all designed to reward those who sell the least protection for the greatest profit/price to the company and the salesman. The principle for consumers is clear: Buy term insurance. Consider using the savings to pay off debt or simply save.

To save money don't buy:

(1) Waiver of premium on your life policy. It is cheaper if you buy a separate single disability income policy.

(2) Accidental death benefit and/or double or triple indemnity. The cost is reasonable, but the odds of collecting are small.

(3) Mortgage insurance or credit life insurance on loans. Costs are excessive, and coverage and choice are restricted.

(4) When you hear the words "group insurance," "low cost," "cash benefits," "valuable protection," "guaranteed issue," "cost is just pennies per day," or "Vets only" on TV, in the newspaper, or in the mail, don't waste your money.

(5) Family riders for spouse and children are usually term insurance. Almost never is it wise to buy life insurance on children. Before buying spouse insurance or family rider, if at all, make sure the primary wage earner is properly protected.

THINK ABOUT HOW TO LEAVE BENEFITS

Did you know that 95% of all beneficiaries of life insurance policies receiving from $100,000 to

$1 million have spent every penny of the proceeds in five years? Those facts, from the life insurance industry, confirm the fact that people don't plan to fail but they fail to plan, and the results are identical. There are many ways to plan so that your insurance proceeds are a blessing instead of a silver-plated curse. Investigate the benefits of having a trust to assist your heirs with the burdensome and dangerous responsibility of decisions involving hundreds of thousands of dollars. A few simple mistakes, which planning could prevent, are the difference between dignity, security, and peace of mind versus disaster, poverty, and a struggle for survival.

Since 85% of husbands pre-decease their wives, it makes excellent sense for husbands to be sure their wives are knowledgeable in the art and science of financial, tax, and estate planning. The average age for a widow today is fifty-three years. Most have no training, experience, or idea of where to begin or what to do. Imagine having to deal with problems for which you have no training or experience while coping with the loss of a mate of twenty, thirty, or forty years. Equip your mate. Not only is investing difficult at best, there are lots of wolves out there disguised as sheep, and bereavement is no time to learn the hard way.

If you own a cash value policy, I suggest you replace it if you:

(1) have existing debts—credit cards, auto loans, or home mortgages;

(2) have a policy based on a pre-1980 mortality table—you can lower your cost per thousand;

(3) own a participating or mutual policy that pays you rebates (called dividends so it is easier to sell);

(4) have more than one policy for the same type of coverage, e.g., life insurance;

(5) can pass a physical and are insurable at standard rates (find out prior to changing any existing policy);

(6) can lower the cost of coverage with a new policy.

Don't replace your policy if you:

(1) are trying to conceal health problems. You will lose your coverage if you lie, omit, or conceal problems;

(2) value the "friend" who sold you the policy more than what you will save;

(3) can't stand the pressure your agent will apply to convince you to keep your policy as is.

Don't look back at what you have lost. Yesterday is a canceled check; tomorrow is a promissory note; only today is legal tender, and only now is negotiable. Hindsight is always 100% accurate. Move ahead—lower your costs or keep the cost level and increase your protection.

PROTECTING YOUR ASSETS

To integrate insurance planning (protecting your assets from unexpected setbacks) with retirement planning (ensuring that those assets will help when you need them), let's look briefly at financial investment reality. Sometimes becoming a millionaire is made to look easy. Save $2,000/year at 10%/year for fifty years, and presto—$2,327,817. But that is before taxes. If we subtract $742,606 for taxes due, our balance is $1,585,211. After adjusting for inflation at 4% per year, we are left with $138,205 in today's inflation-adjusted "real" dollars. You would still have $1,585,211, but it would take $11.47 to buy, fifty years from today, what $1.00 buys today! *The real enemy of long-term financial security is inflation.* Factor inflation into all your long-range planning. To be realistic don't assume you can earn 8%, 10%, 15%, or 20% long range. If your real returns are 0 to 2% per year, after tax and inflation, you're in the top 10% of all investors. There are rare periods like the four years following the stock market crash to a low on October 19, 1987, where you could earn 70% in four years; but those

80

are the exception not the rule. If you had bought stocks in July 1987, and sold them fifty-two months later in November 1991, your total return would have been 11% pre-tax. After inflation and taxes you would have experienced a real, but nondeductible, loss of capital. To be realistic and conservative in planning, *estimate 0 to 2% real return on your investment at best over a five- to ten-year period.*

To help you calculate how much you will need to retire see appendix 2 to:

(1) estimate your life span,

(2) estimate your tax bracket,

(3) estimate your increased need for income due to inflation, and

(4) estimate your pre-tax investment return.

If I were sixty-five today my estimated additional life span would be twenty years, to age eighty-five. Remember, such statistics are based on averages. Averages are correct only half the time. Half of the people age sixty-five die before age eighty-five, and half live beyond age eighty-five. If I were a real pessimist, I would use a thirty-five year life expectancy, to age one hundred. Second, assume that one-third of my income goes for taxes. Third, assume a 4% rate of inflation over my twenty-year average life span. If I earn a 6% rate of return pre-tax and withdraw 6% pre-tax my capital will last for twenty years (study tables). If I extend my lifetime to thirty-four years, I need to earn 6% but withdraw only 4%. Remember, my withdrawal increases 4% each year to offset 4% inflation. From my 4 to 6% withdrawal subtract one-third for taxes, leaving me with 2.67 to 4% after-tax income. That is $26,667 to $40,000 income on a $1,000,000 nest egg. Depending on the size of your company benefit and social security benefits, and the amount of your living expenses, you may require more or less. Real retirement planning requires much more than simply putting $2,000 per year into your IRA.

SAFETY FIRST

Since 1991, with the failure of the eighteenth-largest life insurance company in our nation, Mutual Benefit of New Jersey, much has been written and discussed about the importance of selecting a *safe* insurance company. Following are two charts explaining safety ratings for insurance companies. I strongly suggest that you stay with insurance companies rated highly by at least two of the five rating agencies. For more information contact:

Standard & Poor's	212-208-1527
Moody's	212-553-0377
Duff & Phelps	312-368-3157
A.M. Best	908-439-2200
Weiss	212-208-1527

INSURANCE COMPANY RATINGS

A.M. BEST	STANDARD & POOR'S	MOODY'S	DUFF & PHELPS	DESCRIPTION
A++	AAA	Aaa	AAA	Superior—negligible risk.
A+	AA+	Aa1	AA+	Excellent—modest risk.
A	AA	Aa2	AA	
A-	AA-	Aa3	AA-	
B++	A+	A1	A+	Good—average risk.
B+	A	A2	A	
B	A-	A3	A-	
B-	BBB+	Baa1	BBB+	Adequate—could be vulnerable to economic conditions.
C++	BBB	Baa2	BBB	
C+	BBB-	Baa3	BBB-	
C	BB+	Ba1	BB+	Below average—questionable security.
C-	BB	Ba2	BB	
D	BB-	Ba3	BB-	
E	B+	B1	B+	Poor—high risk.
F	B	B2	B	
	B-	B3	B-	Very poor—may be in default.

S&P, Moody's, and D&P use a different methodology than A.M. Best. Because of those differences, the A.M. Best ratings do not track exactly the same as the other rating agencies.

FOR INVESTMENT PORTFOLIO
RATING OF INSURANCE COMPANIES

NAIC	STANDARD & POOR'S	MOODY'S	DESCRIPTION
Class 1	AAA, AA, A	Aaa, Aa, A	High-grade to medium-grade investment bonds. Capacity to repay principal and interest judged very high (AAA, Aaa) to slightly susceptible to adverse economic conditions (A, A).
Class 2	BBB	Baa	Adequate capacity to repay principal and interest. Slightly speculative.
Class 3	BB	Ba	Speculative. Significant chances that issuer could miss an interest payment.
Class 4	B	B	Issuer has missed one or more interest or principal payments.
Class 5	CCC, CC, C	Caa, Ca, C	Highly speculative to poor-quality issues that are in danger of default. C ratings mean no interest in being paid on the bond at this time.
Class 6	Default	Default	Issuer is in default. Payment of interest of principal is in arrears.

In addition to the assets of the insurance company itself, all states offer some protection to insurance buyers through a State Guarantee Fund. Every insurance company operating within your state contributes to your state's fund. Coverage varies, so check your state's Department of Insurance to see what are the limits of coverage for death benefits, cash values, terms, and conditions. From 1988 to 1991 more than 113 insurance companies defaulted or closed or were forced into bankruptcy. Only deal with legal reserve companies. That's not to panic you—more banks failed in 1991 than all insurance companies since our country's beginning. It will take us thirty years and more than $500 billion to pay for the savings & loan disaster. There is no substitute for doing your homework and dealing only with top-rated, safe companies. Minimize your chance of loss and play it safe.

A very bright friend of mine just learned the hard way that the value of a guarantee is in the fine print. In 1983, he invested into a universal life policy and purchased a $25,000 guaranteed single premium annuity. The annuity guaranteed 10% interest for ten years then market rates or 4%, whichever is better. The company was Baldwin United. My friend's agent assured him he was safe even though Baldwin had fewer assets than liabilities thanks to some unwise investments. My friend will receive nothing for his investment into the universal life policy. He will recover his cost in the annuity in 1996, but he will have no earnings for the fourteen years he has held this investment. If he had examined the ratings, evaluated the underlying portfolio, or done his homework more carefully and thoroughly, he would be more than $75,000 richer today.

INVESTMENT/LIFE INSURANCE

Back at the beginning of the sixties the battle cries were "buy term and invest the difference" versus "you term-ites are twisting and replacing good cash value permanent insurance." Very quickly the industry responded to the loss of cash value policyholders by developing more modern competitive "permanent" products. For decades, permanent insurance offered 2 to 4% rates of return on accumulated cash values. In 1969, the prime rate reached 9%, and cash value policies were being surrendered to invest the proceeds at triple the rates. The first policies were called "interest sensitive whole life." The rates offered on cash values retained a guaranteed floor of 3 to 4%, but current rates reflected much higher market rates. In addition, with improving healthcare and increasing longevity the price of pure insurance had declined.

Today's universal life policies incorporate protection, competitive returns on savings, and flexibility on payments. To give you an idea of prices, here are premiums on three policies offered at various ages by the same company. As you can see, universal life is less expensive than traditional life insurance but more expensive than term insurance. The prices quoted are for a nonsmoking, healthy male.

AGE	WHOLE	UNIVERSAL	TERM
30	$ 875	$ 590	$136
40	1,391	950	163
50	2,311	1,583	320
60	4,717	2,741	610

Our thesis remains: Buy adequate protection at minimum cost. If protection alone is your goal, you are better off at any age purchasing term insurance. We will cover the two reasons to buy cash values protection later: step up in basis and convenience. I strongly recommend that you not consider any cash value product until you have met the six prerequisites, listed on page 93.

Universal life is composed of three components: term insurance, savings, and costs. To analyze a policy it is easiest if all three components are separated so you can see and compare exactly what you are paying for each component. Generally, the term component is more costly than it could be purchased for separately. The savings element is relatively efficient but expensive in terms of expenses, costs, fees, and loads. As with most products or services, you can reduce costs by unbundling combination products. The good news for the salesmen is that universal life pays more commission for selling a higher premium product that is more profitable to the company. The surrender fees, which vary widely from contract, can cost you up to 100% of your premium for a three- to five-year period. You will also find that most policies offer little to no return of cash values the first one to three years.

Universal life is not a short-term investment vehicle. Two major complaints with universal life policies are the deceptive rates of interest and the very long time required to "break even on your investment." Deceptive rates are high because gross rates of interest are quoted before subtracting fees, expenses, and loads. If similar tactics were used by a stock broker or mutual funds salesman, the salesman would lose his license. If I quoted you a 6% rate of interest on a $10,000 investment, you would expect a $600/year return. When you looked at your account and saw a $400 return, you would learn that the gross rate was before expenses of 2%. When comparing contracts make sure you know the "net rate" not "gross rate." To achieve the advertised net rate you must hold your policy a long, long time; ten to twenty years is typical. In the early years there is little or no cash value. To me a required ten-year or longer holding period to break even is excessive.

There are two benefits for universal life—step up in basis for tax-deferred accounts and convenience/flexibility. But, if you surrender the contract, annuitize it, or die and pass the profit to your heirs, you are stuck with a sizable tax bill which at today's rates can approach 50% of your profit. Universal life offers a solution to the problem by easing the tax liability at the death of the owner. For retired or affluent people who want the security of access to cash for an emergency if needed and the ability to pass only assets to heirs without any income tax liability, universal life may be an option.

Other benefits of universal life are convenience, flexibility, and forced savings. To some, these benefits are worth the cost. You can raise or lower the amount of insurance protection subject to certain limits without evidence of insurability, i.e., a medical exam. You can raise or lower your premiums, subject to certain limits. You can also select and plan or have your policy completely paid for at a certain age or within a set time period. Use caution and operate on guaranteed not projected values, or be prepared for unpleasant surprises.

Recently I examined a $100,000 universal life policy issued to a healthy male age forty-five in 1981. Based on projected benefits he planned on eight years of premiums of $2,200 for a total outlay of $17,600. From there on, he was told, no more payments. He had projected cash benefits of $33,000 at age sixty-five. After crunching the numbers, he purchased the policy and relied on the computer-generated illustrations he had verified. His company, Executive Life, was one of more than 113 insurance companies that failed between 1988 and 1991. He learned five lessons the hard way: Projected benefits are not always realized; interest rates can and have declined 70%; state guarantee funds are very difficult to collect if you are alive; premiums on any cash value, universal life, and whole life contracts run to age one hundred as shown in the policy; and mortality rates change over time. His policy was issued on a 1958 mortality table two years after a new table, lowering costs 35%, was available.

Rely on guaranteed benefits, not projections. Read the contract cover to cover. Do your homework. Understand exactly what is and is not covered. My friend accepted a $9,800 nondeductible loss and learned the lesson the hard way. Profit from his experience. If you need protection, buy term insurance. Don't consider cash value products until you are completely debt free, have a spending plan with a surplus, and have adequate savings. Then and only then should you even begin to consider universal life or any other cash value insurance product. Had my friend bought term insurance at the maximum rate shown on page 67, his total outlay would have been $2,604, not $17,600 for the eleven years.

SINGLE PREMIUM LIFE

The idea of making a one-time payment to forever solve your needs for insurance sounds appealing. Companies offer attractive "projected" yields, access to your cash at little or no cost, and the benefits of triple compounding and tax benefits, especially for policies issued prior to August 14, 1984. Billions of dollars have been invested into single pay whole life, universal life, interest sensitive life and other policies with attractive names that have market appeal. These policies should be analyzed as investments using the same principles and ideas as discussed under universal life. If it is protection you need, term insurance remains your lowest cost option. For a detailed analysis see the August 1993 issue of *Consumer Reports*.

SECOND TO DIE POLICIES

If you are fortunate enough to have accumulated substantial assets, you may be aware that federal estate taxes are levied on your death on assets and estates over $600,000. With current estate tax rates of 37 to 60%, the tax can be substantial on large estates. Recognizing the need and people's distaste for taxes has led to the creation of insurance trusts and policies that can be used to pay death taxes. These special policies are called second to die or survivorship policies. They are less expensive to purchase than two individual policies, but they only pay benefits on the second death. Before purchasing this type of policy you should read my book *Saving the Best for Last* (Moody, 1994), which covers many ways to reduce or avoid death taxes without buying insurance. In addition, you should consult a qualified objective, unbiased tax or estate specialist, CPA, or attorney.

VARIABLE LIFE

Variable life policies combine insurance with investments. The value of your investments is not guaranteed like it is with conventional death benefits. Over long periods of time, investments have historically outperformed guaranteed alternatives. Ibbotsen & Associates, an investment research and information service, surveying rates of return from 1926 to today, tell us stocks average 10% per year, bonds 4.7%/year, and inflation 3.3%/year. Whether or not that trend continues in the future remains to be seen. Stocks and bonds also decline in price over time. From July 1987 to October 1987 the stock market plunged from over 2,700 to 1,500, losing 508 points on one day, October 19, 1987. Not all stocks go up in value. Ten thousand dollars invested March 1, 1928, into International Harvester was worth $8,906 sixty-five years later in 1993. An investment can rise, fall, or remain flat. Investments have no guarantee of value at a future date. Even government bonds issued by the Treasury fluctuate in value until maturity, as investors learned during 1978 to 1981 when interest rates tripled and investors lost 44% of their money in long-term Government Bonds. Investments appear to earn more over long or recent time periods but the results are projections and estimates, not guaranteed.

Most variable life is insurance combined with mutual funds. There are 4,000 mutual funds available today with widely varying risks, returns, and objectives. Mutual funds, like any investment, should be carefully analyzed, evaluated, selected, and managed. If you are considering investing, an excellent resource to begin with is Austin Pryor's *Sound Mind Investing* (Moody, 1993). Pryor's book is biblically based and begins by telling you not to invest until you have met the six prerequisites below. Protection of assets is a totally different ball game than accumulation of assets. To accumulate or conserve assets you need a completely new set of guidelines.

I recommend that you not begin to invest if:

(1) you owe any money on your credit cards;

(2) you finance the purchase of cars rather than save and pay cash;

(3) you have a home mortgage;

(4) you do not have three to six months' living wages in savings;

(5) you do not have a spending plan with a surplus.

(6) you have not funded your deductible retirement plan (401K, IRA, Keogh, etc.) to the maximum.

You are always better off paying guaranteed loans (1–2–3 above) than investing. Never invest unless you have adequate savings (4). Don't invest unless your income exceeds your expenses.

FINDING HELP

By now perhaps you are slightly overwhelmed by the scope and complexity of purchasing insurance. Where do you turn for unbiased information and help? Do you need an agent or adviser? Where do you find client-centered counsel? How do you separate good from greedy or incompetent salesmen?

Do not delegate on blind faith your responsibility as a steward of the assets which God has given to your care. In all complex areas of life—including insurance, investing, or finance—step one is to *equip yourself to continue to make better decisions.* This booklet is a first step in education and preparation, but it is not the end of your homework. Over your working life you will spend several hundred thousand dollars of God's money on insurance: medical, disability, home, auto, life, and others. We are both accountable and responsible to function as good stewards. Invest at least ten hours this year rereading, studying, and applying the information in your hands, and you will save yourself hundreds or even thousands of dollars of unnecessary costs. Add up what you are now spending for all insurance this year. Multiply that by 25%. That is a minimum estimate of how much you can reduce your costs this year by applying what you have read! I realize spare time is a rare commodity for all of us, and it is much quicker to select an adviser to whom you can delegate. If you ignore this advice and in blind faith follow the advice of commissioned salesmen, realize that you are still responsible and accountable for the results.

Step one is to equip and educate yourself in the areas of insurance. Step two is to *seek competent counsel.* Too many times I have counseled people who selected advisers because they believed or were told the adviser was a Christian. Being a Christian does not make one a competent insurance specialist. Also, there are wolves in the marketplace disguised as sheep, who devour gullible flocks. There are Christians who wrongly place their needs for commissions above your need to secure adequate protection at minimum cost. There are also good Christians who are incompetent, uninformed, and untrained from the consumer's point of view. Given the choice of equal competence I would much prefer to deal with a Christian, but step number two is to seek competence.

How do you judge competence not being an expert (yet) yourself? A good indicator, though not a guarantee of a competent adviser, is a professional designation. Professional designations like CLU (Certified Life Underwriter), CPCU (Certified Property and Casualty Underwriter), ChFC (Chartered Financial Consultant), or CFP (Certified Financial Planner) are a good beginning. The designation tells you the person is bright enough to pass exams, but it does not tell you the motivation or character of the person. Time in the business is also a good second indicator of competence. Turnover or failure in the insurance business is extremely high during the first few years, so a five year or longer veteran probably has developed competence, or he or she would not have survived. An excellent third indicator is word of mouth referral. Ask for the name of an excellent, client-centered adviser from those you know. Businessmen, CPAs, accountants, relatives, and friends will have had experience; capitalize on their experiences. I personally have eight people I refer to, each specializing in a different area of insurance.

Finally, *establish a relationship and continue to improve your decision making.* Once you master insurance you will learn you can buy by phone or mail exactly what you know you need. Many companies are abandoning insurance agents, offering lower cost products through 800 lines using salaried, not commissioned, consultants. There are also fee only insurance specialists who offer no load or low load products to the consumer. Some offer an offset of commissions against fees; others don't. Finally, there are traditional competent agents with character and values who are compensated solely by commissions. Experience and personal preference will lead you to the right long-term relationship. When in doubt remember and rely on James 1:4: "If any of you lacks wisdom, let him ask of God, who gives to all men generously and without reproach, and it will be given to him."

I encourage you to begin again to study this booklet. Think of this booklet as your resource for insurance. You have already been exposed to 95% of all you need to know to buy adequate protection at minimum cost. The Greek word for *wisdom* used in James 1:4 does not mean knowledge. Knowledge is only potential power. *Wisdom* to the Hebrew minds is applying and living by godly principles. You will benefit most if you commit today to apply what you have learned. Be a more effective steward today of His assets than you have been in the past. Then, one day soon, both of us will stand before our Master and hear, "Well done, good and faithful steward."

APPENDIX 1—
Unisex Life Expectancy (Used by IRS)

This chart should help in your long-range financial planning—how long do your assets need to last? (Remember that these figures are only averages.)

AGE	REMAINING LIFE SPAN	AGE	REMAINING LIFE SPAN	AGE	REMAINING LIFE SPAN
21	60.9	48	34.9	74	13.2
22	59.9	49	34.0	75	12.5
23	59.0	50	33.1	76	11.9
24	58.0	51	32.2	77	11.2
25	57.0	52	31.3	78	10.6
26	56.0	53	34.0	79	10.0
27	55.1	54	29.5	80	9.5
28	54.1	55	28.6	81	8.9
29	53.1	56	27.7	82	8.4
30	52.2	57	26.8	83	7.9
31	51.2	58	25.9	84	7.4
32	50.2	59	25.0	85	6.9
33	49.3	60	24.2	86	6.5
34	48.3	61	23.3	87	6.1
35	47.3	62	22.5	88	5.7
36	46.4	63	21.6	89	5.3
37	45.4	64	20.8	90	5.0
38	44.4	65	20.0	91	4.7
39	43.5	66	19.2	92	4.4
40	42.5	67	18.4	93	4.1
41	41.5	68	17.6	94	3.9
42	40.6	69	16.8	95	3.7
43	39.6	70	16.0	96	3.4
44	38.7	71	15.3	97	3.2
45	37.7	72	14.6	98	3.0
46	36.8	73	13.9	99	2.8
47	35.9				

APPENDIX 2—
How Long Will Your Capital Last?

The following tables show how many years your capital will last at varying rates of withdrawal. For annual withdrawals of equal size, use the first table. The remaining tables assume that you'll take enough extra money each year to keep up with the inflation rate. At 4% inflation, for example, a first-year withdrawal of $5,000 grows to $5,200 the second year, $5,400 the third year, and so on.

To use these tables, choose a likely inflation rate, up to 8%. In the left-hand column, find the percentage of your capital that you will withdraw in the first year. If you withdraw $4,000 from a $100,000 nest egg, for example, you have taken 4%. Read across to the pretax rate of return that you're expecting to earn on your money. Where those lines intersect, you will find the number of years your capital will last. It is assumed that the money is taken at the start of each year. The # symbol means that, at that rate of withdrawal, your capital will never be exhausted. The source for all the tables is John Allen, J.D., of Allen-Warren, Arvada, Colorado.

EQUAL-SIZE WITHDRAWALS

Percent of original capital withdrawn annually	Will last this many years, if invested at the following rates of return										
	4%	5%	6%	7%	8%	9%	10%	11%	12%	13%	14%
2%	#	#	#	#	#	#	#	#	#	#	#
3%	#	#	#	#	#	#	#	#	#	#	#
4%	83	#	#	#	#	#	#	#	#	#	#
5%	35	62	#	#	#	#	#	#	#	#	#
6%	26	32	49	#	#	#	#	#	#	#	#
7%	20	23	28	40	#	#	#	#	#	#	#
8%	17	19	21	25	34	#	#	#	#	#	#
9%	14	15	17	19	23	29	#	#	#	#	#
10%	12	13	14	16	18	25	45	#	#	#	#
11%	11	12	12	13	15	16	18	22	32	#	#
12%	10	10	11	12	12	14	15	17	20	26	#
13%	9	9	10	10	11	12	13	14	15	18	22
14%	8	9	9	9	10	10	11	12	13	14	16
15%	8	8	8	8	9	9	10	10	11	12	13

ASSUMING 2 PERCENT INFLATION

Percent of capital withdrawn in the first year	Will last this many years, if the original withdrawal rises by 2 percent annually and your money is invested at the following rates of return										
	4%	5%	6%	7%	8%	9%	10%	11%	12%	13%	14%
2%	168	#	#	#	#	#	#	#	#	#	#
3%	63	105	#	#	#	#	#	#	#	#	#
4%	34	43	75	#	#	#	#	#	#	#	#
5%	25	29	37	57	#	#	#	#	#	#	#
6%	20	22	26	32	46	#	#	#	#	#	#
7%	17	18	20	23	28	38	#	#	#	#	#
8%	14	15	17	18	21	24	32	#	#	#	#
9%	12	13	14	15	17	19	22	27	52	#	#
10%	11	12	12	13	14	15	17	20	24	35	#
11%	10	10	11	12	12	13	14	16	18	21	28
12%	9	9	10	10	11	12	12	13	15	16	19
13%	8	9	9	9	10	10	11	12	12	13	15
14%	8	8	8	8	9	9	10	10	11	12	13
15%	7	7	8	8	8	8	9	9	10	10	11

ASSUMING 4 PERCENT INFLATION

Percent of capital withdrawn in the first year	Will last this many years, if the original withdrawal rises by 4 percent annually and your money is invested at the following rates of return										
	4%	5%	6%	7%	8%	9%	10%	11%	12%	13%	14%
2%	50	68	151	#	#	#	#	#	#	#	#
3%	33	40	52	96	#	#	#	#	#	#	#
4%	25	28	34	42	69	#	#	#	#	#	#
5%	20	22	25	29	36	53	#	#	#	#	#
6%	17	18	20	22	25	31	43	#	#	#	#
7%	14	15	16	18	20	23	27	35	#	#	#
8%	13	13	14	15	16	18	20	24	30	65	#
9%	11	12	12	13	14	15	17	19	21	26	40
10%	10	10	11	12	12	13	14	15	17	19	23
11%	9	9	10	10	11	11	12	13	14	16	17
12%	8	9	9	9	10	10	11	11	12	13	14
13%	8	8	8	9	9	9	10	10	11	11	12
14%	7	7	8	8	8	8	9	9	10	10	11
15%	7	7	7	7	8	8	8	8	9	9	10

ASSUMING 6 PERCENT INFLATION

Percent of capital withdrawn in the first year	Will last this many years, if the original withdrawal rises by 6 percent annually and your money is invested at the following rates of return										
	4%	5%	6%	7%	8%	9%	10%	11%	12%	13%	14%
2%	35	41	50	67	139	#	#	#	#	#	#
3%	26	29	33	40	51	89	#	#	#	#	#
4%	21	23	25	28	33	42	65	#	#	#	#
5%	17	18	20	22	25	29	35	50	#	#	#
6%	15	16	17	18	20	22	25	30	41	#	#
7%	13	13	14	15	16	18	20	22	26	34	#
8%	11	12	13	13	14	15	16	18	20	23	29
9%	10	11	11	12	12	13	14	15	16	18	21
10%	9	10	10	10	11	12	12	13	14	15	17
11%	8	9	9	9	10	10	11	11	12	13	14
12%	8	8	8	9	9	9	10	10	11	11	12
13%	7	7	8	8	8	9	9	9	10	10	11
14%	7	7	7	7	8	8	8	8	9	9	10
15%	6	6	7	7	7	7	8	8	8	8	9

ASSUMING 8 PERCENT INFLATION

Percent of capital withdrawn in the first year	Will last this many years, if the original withdrawal rises by 8 percent annually and your money is invested at the following rates of return										
	4%	5%	6%	7%	8%	9%	10%	11%	12%	13%	14%
2%	28	32	36	41	50	67	131	#	#	#	#
3%	22	24	26	29	33	40	51	84	#	#	#
4%	18	19	21	23	25	28	33	41	61	#	#
5%	15	16	17	18	20	22	25	28	34	48	#
6%	13	14	15	16	17	18	20	22	25	30	39
7%	12	12	13	13	14	15	16	18	20	22	26
8%	10	11	11	12	13	13	14	15	16	18	20
9%	9	10	10	11	11	12	12	13	14	15	16
10%	9	9	9	10	10	10	11	12	12	13	14
11%	8	8	8	9	9	9	10	10	11	11	12
12%	7	8	8	8	8	9	9	9	10	10	11
13%	7	7	7	7	8	8	8	9	9	9	10
14%	6	7	7	7	7	7	8	8	8	8	9
15%	6	6	6	7	7	7	7	7	7	8	8

APPENDIX 3—
One Dollar Principal
Compounded Annually

END OF YEAR — One dollar principal will have grown to this amount, if invested at the following rates of return

END OF YEAR	2%	4%	6%	8%	10%	12%	15%
1	1.02	1.04	1.06	1.08	1.10	1.12	1.15
2	1.04	1.08	1.12	1.16	1.21	1.25	1.32
3	1.06	1.12	1.19	1.25	1.33	1.40	1.52
4	1.08	1.16	1.26	1.36	1.46	1.57	1.74
5	1.10	1.21	1.33	1.46	1.61	1.76	2.01
6	1.13	1.26	1.41	1.58	1.77	1.97	2.31
7	1.15	1.31	1.50	1.71	1.94	2.21	2.66
8	1.17	1.36	1.59	1.85	2.14	2.47	3.05
9	1.20	1.42	1.68	1.99	2.35	2.77	3.51
10	1.22	1.48	1.79	2.15	2.59	3.10	4.04
11	1.24	1.53	1.89	2.33	2.85	3.47	4.65
12	1.27	1.60	2.01	2.51	3.13	3.89	5.35
13	1.29	1.66	2.13	2.71	3.45	4.36	6.15
14	1.32	1.73	2.26	2.93	3.79	4.88	7.07
15	1.35	1.80	2.39	3.17	4.17	5.47	8.13
16	1.37	1.87	2.54	3.42	4.59	6.13	9.35
17	1.40	1.94	2.69	3.70	5.05	6.86	10.76
18	1.43	2.02	2.85	3.99	5.55	7.69	12.37
19	1.46	2.10	3.02	4.31	6.11	8.61	14.23
20	1.49	2.19	3.20	4.66	6.72	9.64	16.36
21	1.52	2.27	3.39	5.03	7.40	10.80	18.82
22	1.55	2.36	3.60	5.43	8.14	12.10	21.64
23	1.58	2.46	3.81	5.87	8.95	13.55	24.89
24	1.61	2.56	4.04	6.34	9.84	15.17	28.62

END OF YEAR	One dollar principal will have grown to this amount, if invested at the following rates of return						
	2%	4%	6%	8%	10%	12%	15%
25	1.64	2.66	4.29	6.84	10.83	17.00	32.91
26	1.67	2.77	4.54	7.39	11.91	19.04	37.85
27	1.71	2.88	4.82	7.98	13.11	21.32	43.53
28	1.74	2.99	5.11	8.62	14.42	23.88	50.06
29	1.78	3.11	5.41	9.31	15.86	26.74	57.57
30	1.81	3.24	5.74	10.06	17.44	29.95	66.21
31	1.85	3.37	6.08	10.86	19.19	33.55	76.14
32	1.88	3.50	6.45	11.73	21.11	37.58	87.56
33	1.92	3.64	6.84	12.67	23.22	42.09	100.69
34	1.95	3.79	7.25	13.69	25.54	47.14	115.80
35	2.00	3.94	7.68	14.78	28.10	52.79	133.17
36	2.04	4.10	8.14	15.96	30.91	59.13	153.15
37	2.08	4.26	8.63	17.24	34.00	66.23	176.12
38	2.12	4.43	9.15	18.62	37.40	74.17	202.54
39	2.16	4.61	9.70	20.11	41.14	83.08	232.92
40	2.21	4.80	10.28	21.72	45.25	93.05	267.86
41	2.25	4.99	10.90	23.46	49.78	104.21	308.04
42	2.30	5.19	11.55	25.33	54.76	116.72	354.14
43	2.34	5.40	12.25	27.36	60.24	130.72	407.38
44	2.39	5.61	12.98	29.55	66.26	146.41	468.49
45	2.44	5.84	13.76	31.92	72.89	163.98	538.76
46	2.49	6.07	14.59	34.47	80.17	183.66	619.58
47	2.54	6.31	15.46	37.23	88.19	205.70	712.52
48	2.59	6.57	16.39	40.21	97.01	230.39	819.40
49	2.65	6.83	17.37	43.42	106.71	258.03	942.31
50	2.69	7.10	18.42	46.90	117.39	289.00	1083.65

APPENDIX 4—
One Dollar Per Annum
Compounded Annually

END OF YEAR	One dollar per year will have grown to this amount, if invested at the following rates of return						
	2%	4%	6%	8%	10%	12%	15%
1	1.02	1.04	1.06	1.08	1.10	1.12	1.15
2	2.06	2.12	2.18	2.24	2.31	2.37	2.47
3	3.12	3.24	3.37	3.50	3.64	3.77	3.99
4	4.20	4.41	4.63	4.86	5.10	5.35	5.73
5	5.31	5.63	5.97	6.33	6.71	7.11	7.75
6	6.43	6.89	7.39	7.92	8.48	9.08	10.06
7	7.58	8.21	8.89	9.63	10.43	11.29	12.72
8	8.75	9.58	10.49	11.48	12.57	13.77	15.78
9	9.95	11.00	12.18	13.48	14.93	16.54	19.30
10	11.17	12.48	13.97	15.64	17.53	19.65	23.34
11	12.41	14.02	15.86	17.97	20.38	23.13	28.00
12	13.68	15.62	17.88	20.49	23.52	27.02	33.35
13	14.97	17.29	20.01	23.21	26.97	31.39	39.50
14	16.29	19.02	22.27	26.15	30.77	36.27	46.58
15	17.64	20.82	24.67	29.32	34.94	41.75	54.71
16	19.01	22.69	27.21	32.75	39.54	47.88	64.07
17	20.41	24.64	29.90	36.45	44.59	54.74	74.83
18	21.84	26.67	32.76	40.44	50.15	62.43	87.21
19	23.30	28.77	35.78	44.76	56.27	71.05	101.44
20	24.78	30.96	38.99	49.42	63.00	80.69	117.81
21	26.39	33.24	42.39	54.45	70.40	91.50	136.63
22	27.84	35.61	45.99	59.89	78.54	103.60	158.27
23	29.42	38.08	49.81	65.76	87.49	117.15	183.16
24	31.03	40.64	53.86	72.10	97.34	132.33	211.79

END OF YEAR	2%	4%	6%	8%	10%	12%	15%
25	32.67	43.31	58.15	78.95	108.18	149.33	244.71
26	34.34	46.08	62.70	86.35	120.09	168.37	282.56
27	36.03	48.96	67.52	94.33	133.20	189.69	326.10
28	37.79	51.96	72.63	102.96	147.63	213.58	376.16
29	39.57	55.08	78.05	112.28	163.49	240.33	433.74
30	41.38	58.32	83.80	122.34	180.94	270.29	499.95
31	43.23	61.70	89.88	133.21	200.13	303.84	576.10
32	45.11	65.20	96.34	144.95	221.25	341.42	663.66
33	47.03	68.85	103.18	157.62	244.47	383.52	764.36
34	48.99	72.65	110.43	171.31	270.02	430.66	880.17
35	50.99	76.59	118.12	186.10	298.12	483.46	1013.37
36	53.03	80.70	126.26	202.07	329.03	542.59	1166.49
37	55.11	84.97	134.90	219.31	363.04	608.83	1342.62
38	57.24	89.40	144.05	237.94	400.44	683.01	1545.16
39	59.40	94.02	153.76	258.05	441.59	766.09	1778.09
40	61.61	98.82	164.04	279.78	486.85	859.14	2045.95
41	63.86	103.81	174.95	303.24	536.63	963.35	2353.99
42	66.16	109.01	186.50	328.58	591.40	1080.08	2708.24
43	68.50	114.41	198.75	355.94	651.64	1210.81	3115.63
44	70.89	120.02	211.74	385.50	717.90	1357.23	3584.12
45	73.33	125.87	225.50	417.42	790.79	1521.21	4122.89
46	75.82	131.94	240.09	451.90	870.97	1704.88	4742.48
47	78.35	138.26	255.56	489.13	959.17	1910.58	5455.00
48	80.94	144.83	271.95	529.34	1056.18	2140.98	6274.40
49	83.58	151.66	289.33	572.77	1162.90	2399.01	7216.71
50	86.27	158.77	307.75	619.67	1280.29	2688.02	8300.37

END OF YEAR — One dollar per year will have grown to this amount, if invested at the following rates of return